Published by C.L.W. Publishing
The Old Vicarage, Boxted, Colchester CO4 5ST

First published
November 2006

ISBN 0-9553880-0-7
ISBN 978-09553880-0-2

Boxted

PORTRAIT OF AN ENGLISH VILLAGE

Douglas Carter

Profits in aid of

Boxted Church Support Trust

EACH ONE OF US HAS A KIND OF PRIVATE VIEW of the villages which surround our particular town or village. We know a little of their history and are familiar with their scenery. Our experience extends into them but soon discovers that though they are part of our native territory they are strongly individual and our knowledge of them is too limited for us to see them as much more than a cluster of old and new houses round an ancient church. Mercifully there are guidebooks to most of them, and what a delight they are. I have collected them all my life, and have myself written one or two. This one is superb, a guidebook and a half, one might say. For it tutors the reader all along, tying in Boxted's history with England's history and showing how a little rural community had a role in mighty events. It is both scholarly and intimate, as a good guide should be, and parts of it could serve as essential information about many a village.

My familiarity with Boxted grew out of boyhood walks and cycle rides in the Stour Valley, and from the hospitality of Robert and Natalie Bevan at Boxted House. I was often there with my friend John Nash R. A. and other Suffolk/Essex artists and writers. 'Going to Boxted' was something to look forward to and I never failed to wander off to catch a glimpse of the river or explore the church. John Constable's great-great-grandfather, William Constable, was a Boxted man and the artist would sometimes walk over to the village via the 'Langham Hills'. John Nash painted watercolours of Boxted Mill and of the patches of Boxted woodland, loving the untypical steepness of this fraction of East Anglia, with its deep ditches and complex lanes.

The other Boxted association which continues to excite my imagination is of course the role the village played in the extraordinary migration to Massachusetts Bay in 1630. To think that there are some old winding streets in Boston which still follow the tracks made by the cattle of the first settlers in America, most of them from Puritan Suffolk and Essex, and some from Boxted, including the Rector himself, George Phillips. I thought of the huge Essex wagons loaded with household goods, nails, saws, farm stock, including seedcorn, and the courageous families setting off to Southampton and the Atlantic. 'Boxted: Portrait of an English village' is the perfect guide to a place which helped to change history and whose beautiful river landscape as seen by Constable revolutionised English art. The authors understand the value of minutiae and detail, and of simple explanation. They show how village work patterns and belief do become, in this instance, the formative patterns of a new nation. Due to a number of historic religious happenings and spiritual forces this border village will always be associated with the fountain of New England. The authors introduce one to it as their own home, knowing everything about it and able to make its architecture, characters and climate live for us.

Bottengoms, Wormingford

Introduction

THIS BOOK IS A COMPREHENSIVE and copiously illustrated history of Boxted, a small Essex village situated some five miles to the north of Colchester, lying partly in Dedham Vale, and 'Constable Country'.

The name Boxted is thought to come from the Saxon 'Bocchestaeda' which means 'the place of the beech trees'. The land is level in the South, and to the North there are gentle valleys with small streams running down to the River Stour, the Essex-Suffolk county boundary. The parish covers an area of some 3,177 acres, the second largest parish in Essex.

EVIDENCE OF PREHISTORIC SETTLEMENT has been found: circular cropmarks, the lines of ditches and field boundaries with traces of what may have been a Iron/Bronze Age henge can be seen from the air, while Neolithic flint tools have been unearthed by farming operations. It seems possible there was a Neolithic settlement in Boxted dating from 4,000 to 2,000 BC - a long time ago!

THE ROMANS were present in the village for almost 100 years and certainly farmed the land, though most of the work was probably done by the Trinovantes, a local tribe. There was a Roman villa in a neighbouring village, and probably another in Boxted though any remains have been obscured by a more recent farm site. There is Roman brick in the construction of St. Peter's church. The Romans left the area sometime in the 5th Century AD.

THE JUTE AND SAXON invasions came next, probably betweeen 450 and 500 AD. The two manor houses, Boxted Hall, and Rivers Hall are thought to be of Saxon origin and may overlay Roman farm sites. The first Christian church is also believed to have been Saxon.

When the Normans came to Boxted, shortly after the Conquest, they replaced the lords at both Boxted Hall and Rivers Hall with their own men, establishing their own system of government and economic control, which became known as the Feudal System. This lasted for the next 200 years, probably longer.

The mediaeval era saw the demise of the Feudal System and the establishment of Common Law. In Boxted two events dominated village history; the Black Death, and the arrival of Flemish weavers. The Black Death was responsible for the deaths of 50 percent of the village population, leaving insufficient survivors to continue working the predominantly arable land, two thirds of which had reverted to pasture grazed by large numbers of sheep, a major change in local farming practice. This coincided with the arrival in England with weavers from the Low Countries, victims of religious persecution, and economic migrants. Two of these weavers settled in Boxted, which led to the establishment of the cloth trade in the village and gave Boxted many years of prosperity.

Tudor and Stuart times: a period of instability and much change. The Reformation led to an increase in Nonconformist belief which caused the persecution of, at first protestants, and then catholics. With the establishment of the Church of England a period of stability returned. Nevertheless, many parishioners felt unsafe and decided to emigrate to the 'New World', including Boxted's vicar George Phillips. Later the village became embroiled in the Civil War, particularly the 1648 uprising.

In the period following the first Civil War, 'witch fever' became endemic due to extreme Protestantism. Matthew Hopkins, an unsuccessful lawyer from nearby Manningtree, became the self-appointed 'Witchfinder General'. Many innocent men and women were denounced by him as warlocks or witches and were hanged.

The Stour Valley looking towards Boxted from Stoke by Nayland. Rivers Hall Long barn is on the left (June 2006).

WILLIAM AND THE HANOVERIANS. Boxted, like many other villages, once again stood at the threshold of change. The cloth trade which had once brought such prosperity to the village had declined. The rapid expansion of towns and cities fuelled increased demand for food and the consequent agricultural expansion. Boxted benefited from this, and the resulting prosperity led to the creation of new small businesses and the building of new houses. Indeed, there was a general feeling of well-being in the village.

THE NINTEENTH CENTURY was a period of mixed fortunes; Boxted Heath was enclosed and subdivided into a geometric pattern of fields which were then sold at public auction. To gain access, roads were laid out dividing the main areas into blocks. Hence we have Straight Road in the centre connecting the village to Colchester, with secondary roads leading off it. During the period of agricultural prosperity, one of the country's leading and most innovative farmers, William Fisher Hobbs, lived at Boxted Lodge. In 1825 the village population had increased to 935 but dropped to 680 by 1901. In 1863 Boxted boasted 25 farmers, six publicans, two millers, six shopkeepers, two wheelwrights, one baker, one blacksmith, one harness maker, three shoemakers, five academies of learning, one butcher and a post office. Ten years later, and in stark contrast, the list of business read 12 farmers, five publicans, one miller, one wheelwight, one baker, one blacksmith, one harness maker, one private school, one butcher and a post office. Unemployment is recorded as 140 persons and 15 paupers. This disastrous decline in farming fortunes was mostly due to cheap imports of grain from North America.

During the 19th Century there was a great increase in the amount and variety of machinery used on the farms. As well as the self-binder for cutting and tying the corn into sheaves, there were steam engines and stationary threshing sets to thresh the corn and steam ploughs to help till the land. This 'progress' led to a decrease in the number of workers required on the land, and inevitably resulted in an exodus of villagers to the towns and an increase in unemployment.

In 1894, the 'Parish Vestry', the lowest tier of local government, was replaced with an elected 'Parish Council'. Towards the end of the century Britain was involved in the South African war in which several Boxted men served.

MODERN TIMES. The turbulent 20th Century of British history witnessed more change than in the preceding five centuries. Boxted was no exception. In 1906 the Salvation Army bought 400 acres of land on Boxted Heath and launched a smallholding scheme to put 'landless people on peopleless land'. The estate was divided up into five and six acre blocks each with its own semi-detached house. Many of the first smallholders came from the East End of London, but in spite of help from the Salvation Army, most found it difficult to pay their way. The scheme was wound up in 1916 and the estate taken over and administered by the County Council.

The great war of 1914-18 didn't leave Boxted untouched. Many local men answered the call to arms, 16 of whom lost their lives. After the war the pace of change accelerated. Local council houses were built, the electricity supply was extended and mains water became available to most houses. However, the increasing mechanisation of agriculture led to the demise of the heavy horse and increasing unemployment. Fruit farming was introduced to Boxted at Hill Farm. It was labour intensive and saved the village from the worst effects of unemployment which accompanied the serious decline of agriculture between the wars. Vegetable production by local market gardens also thrived and provided jobs.

In 1939 the country was again at war with Germany and many local men enlisted. With attacks from the air by the Luftwaffe, and the construction of airfields throughout East Anglia, one built locally to carry the attack back to Hitler's Germany, villagers felt they were in the forefront of the battle. Post 1945 many more houses were built and mains drainage provided for much of the village. The road system was improved, but today is inadequate due to the enormous expansion of road traffic.

CONTENTS

Images Index

We are grateful to all the many people who took the archive photographs in this book whom we cannot acknowledge.

Most modern photographs are credited in the captions.

Where not credited, photography is by: Adrian Arnold, Hugh Large or Judith Large.

ACKNOWLEDGEMENTS

Written by
Douglas Carter

Compiled by
Adrian Arnold

Designed by
Hugh Large

Published by
Jeremy Carter
Hugh Large
Stephen Whybrow

Proof reading by
Anne Carter
Jeremy Carter
David Cross
Judith Large
Jonathan Minter
Michaela Quah
Helen Wenham
Stephen Whybrow

Photography by
Adrian Arnold
Kim Barclay
Will Barclay
Lucinda Douglas-Menzies
Hugh Large
Judith Large
John Minter
Robert Thompson

CHAPTER ONE

THE history of Boxted village

THE VILLAGE OF BOXTED lies some 5 miles north of Colchester. The parish covers 3,177 acres bordered on the North by the River Stour and on the south by the Salary Brook, a tributary of the River Colne. The eastern and western boundaries lie against the parishes of Great Horkesley and Langham respectively. The land rises from ten metres above sea level to 45 metres on the ridge near the church. The soil is a largely glacial drift of sand, gravel and loam with the underlying London clay exposed in the valleys of the Stour and its tributaries.

Straight Road, Boxted.

No main roads pass through the parish, although a locally important ridgeway runs from Great Horkesley to the village. The roads across Boxted Heath including Straight Road were laid out when the Heath was enclosed (see short history of Boxted). The cart track from Boxted to Colchester extended from Oatland, east of the Cross Inn, along the line of Cage Lane, west of the Methodist Church to Langham Road, thence onwards to the east of Colchester.

The name Boxted is thought to be derived from the Saxon name Bocchestaeda meaning the 'place of the beech trees'. For most of its history the village was an agricultural community, although in the 16th Century the weaving of woollen cloth was a major occupation of the inhabitants. Today it is largely a dormitory village with a little light industry. The open land is still farmed, albeit with a greatly reduced labour force.

Prehistoric and Roman times

IT SEEMS LIKELY THAT THERE WAS A NEOLITHIC settlement south of the River Stour

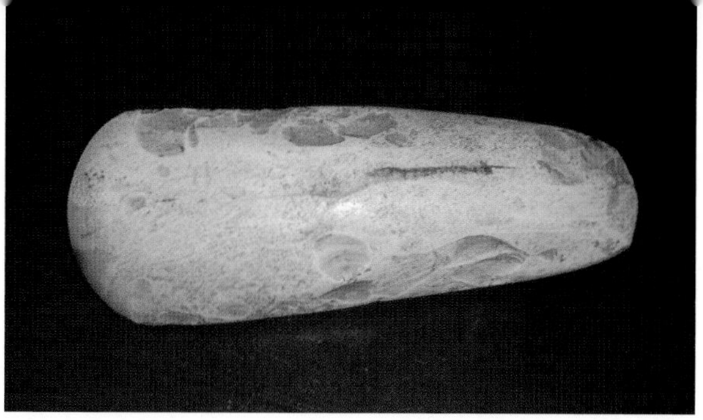

Stone age axe head found in Boxted. Mr Tom Whiteman, of Cage Lane spotted it in 1945 whilst ploughing a field for his father Sydney, at Noakes Farm behind the Methodist Chapel.

between Boxted Hall and the river. Many fine stone arrowheads and tools found across the River Stour at Nayland are now in the care of the Cambridge University Museum. The early settlement seemed to progress south from the Stour rather than north from Colchester. Cropmarks such as ring ditches, trackways and possible field systems as well as other scattered finds, suggest social activity beside Boxted Hall along the Stour west of Boxted Mill and on the high ground around Rivers Hall. The earliest settlement at Boxted may have been a clearing on high ground overlooking the river.

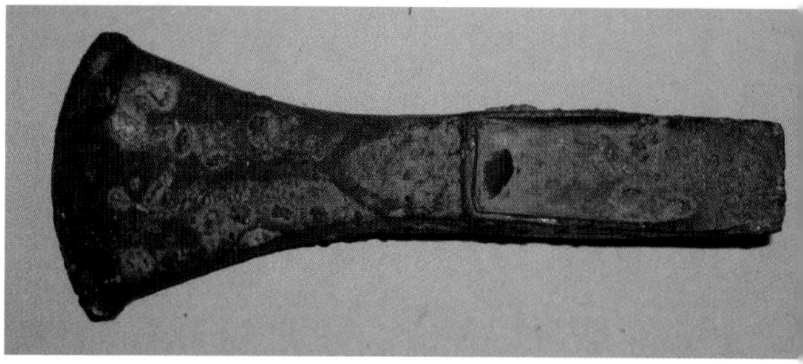

Bronze palstave or axe head found at Boxted Hall thought to date from 1500BC

Although the early Neolithic people were mainly hunter-gatherers, they were followed by the first farmers, who possessed the ability to cultivate the land and to domesticate farm animals.

In 600 BC Southern England was invaded by the Celts. This Aryan race had migrated westwards from the Caspian Sea to infiltrate the whole of Europe, occupying East Anglia by 300 BC. The area lying north of the Thames to a line roughly joining Ipswich and Cambridge was occupied by the tribe of Trinovantes, with the Iceni tribe ruling north of this area. The Trinovantine Celts who probably inhabited Boxted, held the advantage over the Neolithic people with their ability to work in bronze and iron.

The Romans first set foot in Britain in 55 BC (or BCE), but full conquest was not achieved for another 88 years. In 42 AD (CE) Cunobelin, Roman Colchester governed an area north to Stowmarket, west as far as Reading, and probably included Kent. The land in Boxted was certainly farmed by Romans who left behind a legacy suffered by farmers to this day. They introduced the common weed Fat Hen which they cultivated, grinding its seed into flour.

The land in Boxted was certainly farmed by Romans who left behind a legacy suffered by farmers to this day.

Roman organisation brought peace and stability to the region with the Celts working in partnership with the invaders. Unfortunately in 61 AD the Romans and the Iceni tribes fell out, and while the legions were dispatched to Wales, Queen Boudicca and the Iceni laid waste to Colchester. They are believed to have forded the Stour at Boxted in order to surprise the garrison by attacking from the East. The decline of the Roman empire in the 5th Century, saw the withdrawal of their legions from Boxted.

Opposite: The fields of Rivers Hall Farm in the Stour Valley (2006).

St. Peter's Church, completed sometime between 1090 and 1130, consisted of the tower, nave and chancel all under a thatched roof.

Saxons and Normans 410 – 1154

THE ANGLO-SAXON OCCUPATION OF BRITAIN took well over 150 years to complete. When the early Saxons (Jutes) came to occupy the south-east of the country, the rest of the country was governed by the Roman trained Celts. The Saxons discarded the Roman civilisation as it was unsuited to their essentially agricultural communities, and it was only after their conversion to Christianity that the Saxon civilisation began to improve.

The exact date of the arrival of Saxons to Boxted cannot be established, but it was probably between 449 and 500 AD. Both Boxted manors, Boxted Hall and Rivers Hall, are probably of Saxon origin, and one if not both may stand upon previous Roman farm sites. The Domesday Book of 1085 shows the Saxon Lord of Boxted Hall to be Aluric and that of Rivers Hall, Grim. The Saxons built a watermill at Boxted beside the crossing of the Stour to Stoke by Nayland,

and raised the first church on the site of St. Peter's Church today. Agriculture was the prime occupation of the Saxons who were now calling themselves English. Crops of oats and barley were grown on rotation in three large fields of which strips or allotments were apportioned annually to ceorls or freemen not tied.

While we attribute the early road system to the Romans, the Saxons constructed many of their own. In Boxted, the east-west route from Great Horkesley to Langham and Stratford St. Mary is credited to the early English.

When a tenant or copyholder died, a tax called a 'heriot' was levied on his goods and chattels.

The Viking raids on the east coast never penetrated as far as Boxted.

The defeat of the English by the Normans in 1066 had little immediate effect on the village. Earl Eustace, who held his court at Witham, was given the Boxted Hall demense when the Normans eventually arrived in Boxted. At Rivers Hall Arturus supplanted Lord Grim. All land was now in the gift of the King to whom the Lords owed allegiance. Likewise the tenants had feudal obligations to their lord. When a tenant or copyholder died, a tax called a 'heriot' was levied on his goods and chattels but tenants also enjoyed certain privileges such as the right to cut 'fyrebote, hedgebote and wallbote,' being timber for the fire, fence and home repairs. Earl Eustace rebuilt the manor house of Boxted Hall, but the watermill had fallen into disrepair and Arturus built a new mill further downriver near the site of the present day waterworks.

In the late 11th Century, cultivation was probably concentrated in the north-east and north-west of the parish where the demesnes of Boxted Hall and Rivers Hall later lay. Boxted Hall's woodland for 300 swine was probably further south next to Cestrewald in 1086, at which time woodland clearance was in progress.

Mediaeval Times 1154 – 1485

DURING THIS PERIOD, FUSION between the English and the Normans became complete. There were more sophisticated systems of religious and civil government, social life began to break free from feudal control and towns became more important as trade and industry grew. On the one hand this was a time of incessant warfare, social and religious revolt, political failure and industrial unrest, while on the other it witnessed human thought revitalised, the establishment of Common Law and the acceptance of English as our native tongue.

MEDIAEVAL COURTS

These were of two kinds: the court baron and the court leet. Both spring from the early middle ages. Each manor (an estate granted from a superior lord or even the king himself) belonged to a 'Lord of the Manor', and it was his responsibility to organize the life of the estate for his own profit, and the rights of the workers living there. This was done through the court baron, which in the early years of the mediaeval period met every two or three weeks. The court dealt with such matters as the transfer of land, the organization of common fields and meadows, the abatement of nuisances (defective hedges, blocking of paths, straying beasts, etc) and anything concerning the occupation of the inhabitants, which in most manors were agricultural. The Steward, who ran the court of the lord, kept a watchful eye over the Lord's rights, including rentals, heriots and boon work.

Every county in England was divided in to 'hundreds', small administrative areas dating from Saxon times. A modern parallel would be a District Council. The hundred court consisted of representatives from all its manors and had jurisdiction over petty offence and civil affairs, which courts baron had not. Lords who found this irksome could apply to the Crown to have the rights of/...

The Long Barn, Rivers Hall farm, (page 59) with the Stour Valley behind. (W. Barclay 2004).

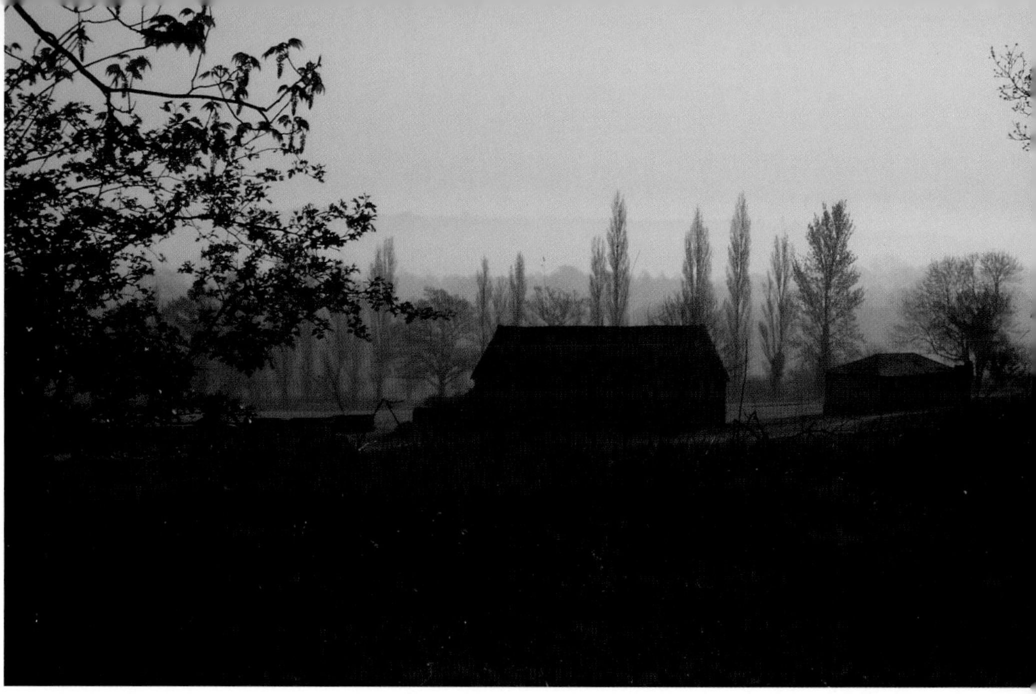

Law of the land

THE LORD OF BOXTED HELD 'view of frankpledge' in 1303 when the bailiff of the honour of Boulogne had two shillings from its profits.

Frankpledge, from the Latin 'francum plegium', is an early English institution consisting of an association for mutual security whose members were perpetual bail for each other. The custom whereby the inhabitants of a district were responsible for any crime or injury committed by one of their number, is old and widespread; it prevailed in England before the Norman Conquest and is an outcome of the earlier principle whereby this responsibility rested on kinship. Thus a law of Edgar (d. 975) says "and let every man so order that he have a 'borh' (a word meaning surety, pledge or obligation), and let the 'borh' then bring and hold him to every justice; and if any one then do wrong and run away, let the 'borh' bear that which he ought to bear"; and a law of Canute about 1030 says "and that every one be brought into a hundred and in 'borh', and let the 'borh' hold and lead him to every plea". About this time these societies, each having its headman, were called 'frithborhs', or 'peace-borhs'. The Normans replaced the Anglo-Saxon word by frankpledge. But the history of the frankpledge proper begins later than the time of the Norman Conquest. The laws, which although called the laws of Edward the Confessor, were not drawn up until about 1130, contain a clause about 'frithborhs' which decrees that in every place societies of ten men shall be formed for mutual security and reparation. Prior to this date, William the Conqueror had ordered that every one who wished to be regarded as free must be in a pledge, and that the pledge must hold and bring him to justice if he commits any offence. The laws of Henry I ordered every person of substance over 12 years of age to be enrolled in a frankpledge. This association of 10, or as it often was at a later date 12 men, was also called a tithing, or 'decima', and in the north of England was known as 'tenmanne tale'.

/... the hundred court applied to them for use in their own manors. Such an additional court in a manor we call the 'court leet'. It met twice a year. It did not take long for a lord to fuse his court baron and court leet into one court, meeting only twice annually.

The court leet was also called the 'cruia magna' or Great Court or the View of Frankpledge.

In 1235 Boxted Hall had foresters in charge of its woods, and before 1258, the Crown had rights to the oaks in the woodland. In 1265 the Boxted Hall demesne consisted of 120 acres of arable, 20 acres of pasture, seven acres of meadow and five acres of woodland. By 1325, the arable land had increased to 250 acres, although flooding restricted sowing to 192 acres and ruined the seven acres of meadow. (Recorded in Boxted Hall.) At this time the woodland had been converted to heath by the removal of timber. In 1347 the Rivers Hall estate comprised 160 acres of arable, 40 acres of meadow, 30 acres of pasture and 40 acres of woodland.

> Henry I ordered every person of substance over 12 years of age to be enrolled in a frankpledge.

Boxted shared both the good and the bad of this period. The Black Death ravaged the village in 1348-9 and the decay of feudalism almost ruined the two village manors. In 1437 an inquest on the Boxted Hall estate described the manor as 'One hall of two chambers, two granges and one stable – worth nothing as broken down and ruinous'. (Recorded in Boxted Hall.) Following the Black Death there were insufficient survivors to cultivate the land and a large part went back to pasture. This proved something of a disguised blessing, for the sheep grazing these pastures provided the wool that was to revive Boxted's fortunes. By 1450 Boxted was a 'Towne' of sufficient importance to warrant an Act of Parliament to promote the weaving industry.

Some of the earliest family names begin to appear in records of 1218 onwards. Names such as

A view of the Stour Valley. (W. Barclay 2004).

PROCESSES IN WOOL PRODUCTION

The sheep would be gathered together to be washed in a shallow river, at a specially dammed place. They would then be left to dry naturally. In early summer they would be clipped with iron shears, and the wool spread out to be picked over, to clean it further. The cleaned fleeces were then combed. The combs consisted of two or more rows of iron teeth, set in a wooden base, with a wooden handle placed at right angles to it. Pairs of combs were used,with one comb holding a lock of fleece, while the other was used to comb down over it. Wool during this period was NOT carded, NOR combed with teasels! Combed wool gives long smooth 'tops' of wool which when spun give a tightly twisted hard yarn. This is worsted - a long wool that originated in Worsted, Norfolk.

The grease would be left in some of the wool if the finished product would need to be waterproof, or the wool was scoured, using urine, to remove the grease.

Spinning was an activity carried out by every able-bodied member of the family in every spare moment. Prodigious amounts of yarn are needed to make cloth, (eight miles for one tunic). Also bear in mind that the single spun thread would have to be 'plied' or twisted together with two /...

John Fitz-Earnest, William Fitz-Henry, William Briton and Gilbert de Boxtede who held a field called Bacon's Acre – perhaps the same site as Bacon's Piece on Workhouse Hill. Adam de Wenlak paid a rent of 'one clove of a gillyflower' at Easter. By the 14th Century village names had become more anglicised, with occupational and location names more evident; Stephen the smith, Hugh of the park, Phillip at Melne, Clement att Pond and Christine atte fen. Topographical names such as Wood, Brook, Fen, Pond, Hill and Down suggest a dispersed settlement early in the 14th Century. John at Heath (1250), Geoffrey at Heath (1272) and a further John at Heath (1327) probably lived on the edge of the heath. Spelling was variable to say the least, with differences being found in a single document. The Task Roll of 1450 include some of the most enduring names of the village; Aubrey, Messing, Downe, Perryman, Warner and Spede all appear in this document.

By 1450 Boxted was a 'Towne' of sufficient importance to warrant an Act of Parliament to promote the weaving industry.

The village was first recorded in 1460 when a house to the east of the churchyard was divided into four dwellings or shops, and by 1586 the village boasted some important houses. The hamlets of Bowrede (Bowered) or Cheshunts Green, east of the village, and Workhouse Hill, near the heath, existed by the 16th Century.

Trade prospered during mediaeval times and Boxted produced not only enough food for itself, but enough to sell and export to the Continent. In 1296, 305 sheep were exported to the Continent from the villages via Colchester. By 1301 this total had risen to 1100. Edward III eventually banned the export of wool to the Continent. This and religious persecution led to many Flemish weavers coming to England.

Between 1378 and 1379 the black death destroyed 45% of the village population; this led to a change in farming practice: sheep, mostly Norfolk Longhorns, were grazed on the village pastures, and Boxted prospered with the aid of the Flemish weavers. Weaving sheds were built near the river and tenterfields were established by the watermill. The field still called Woolpit may have contained the wool washing ponds. Some of the most expensive woollen cloth was made in Boxted. A cloth called Russetts was the type generally produced in quantity but Boxted produced the expensive Blue Medleys which were exported to Vatican City.

With the Middle Ages drawing to a close, Boxted was enjoying relative prosperity while many areas of the country were being ravaged by civil war and social revolt.

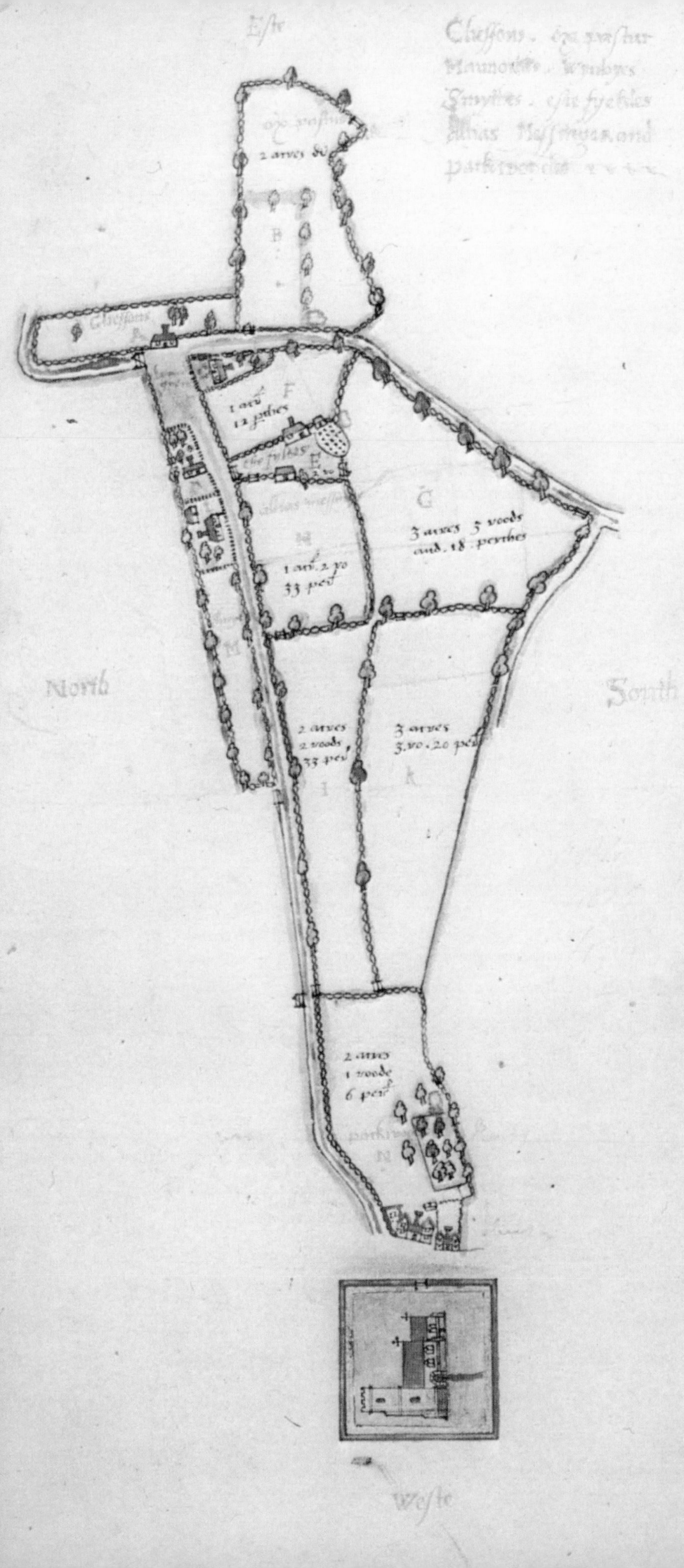

Map of Church Street, 1586 showing Chessons (Cheshunts) at the top (East) and St Peter's Church at the bottom (West). From the Walker survey, Rivers Hall.

/... or more other strands, to make it strong enough to use on the loom.

After the cloth was woven, it would be removed from the loom, and soaked in water to settle the weave. It would then be stretched out to dry sometimes pulled tight on hooks (tenterhooks). When almost dry, it would be bashed with hunks of teasels fastened to a wooden holder.

The resulting 'nap' was then trimmed to a uniform length. Not every piece of cloth received all of these treatments. Many would have been sold straight from the loom.

Tudors and Stuarts 1485 – 1688

THIS PROSPERITY WAS NOT TO LAST. In 1490 sheep scab spread from Suffolk to the local flocks, and by 1495 wool production in Boxted had almost ceased, although some weaving continued using imported wool from Yorkshire.

Agricultural production in the village suffered a series of droughts and storms which resulted in poor harvests. The harvest of 1572 was so bad in the Colchester area that Cardinal Wolsey visited the town to ensure that wheat was not being stockpiled by the wealthy. The years 1594 to 1597 saw four successive bad harvests when grain had to be brought in from Norfolk to feed the local population. During this famine the price of wheat rose from 23 shillings a quarter to 42 shillings. With the wage of a farm labourer at the time averaging two pence per day, poverty and hunger were constant worries. Malnutrition, especially among the young, contributed to the high mortality rate of the influenza and typhus epidemic of 1557 to 1559. As if this were not enough, bubonic plague returned to the village in 1603, fortunately without the disastrous consequences of 1348.

By 1503 the Rivers Hall estate had expanded to 200 acres of arable, 140 acres of meadow, 100 acres of pasture, 100 acres of woodland and 300 acres of heath. 60 years later, in 1563, the estate had expanded further to 363 acres of arable and pasture, 103 acres of meadow and about 55 acres of woodland. There was also a warren of about 10 acres.

Locals believed the oldest elm tree in Essex was growing on Rivers Hall farm. Inevitably it was one of the many victims of Dutch Elm disease in 1974. (J. Minter).

This is not to say that Boxted did not have some good years under Tudor rule. There were three market days in Colchester each week to which the yeoman farmers brought their produce for sale or export to London. The silting of the shipping channels in the river Colne prevented export to the continental ports.

DRY MEASURES
Two gallons = one peck
Four pecks = one bushel
Three bushels = one sack or bag
Eight bushels = one quarter
36 bushels = chaldron
12 sacks = one chaldron
Five quarters = one load
The gallon was mentioned in Piers Plowman in 1342 and the peck has been used since the 14th Century.

With the end of the feudal system and the letting of land to the yeoman farmers, many new farmhouses and cottages were built in the village. Farmhouses such as Hill House, Pond House and Barritts, and cottages like Holly Cottage, Lords Grove, Box Cottage and Wig Cottage were all built in the 16th century. It is believed that the village alehouse at Boxted Cross was built in 1556 and started trading in 1560. Excessive intake of ale by some villagers led to the erection of a cage on the small green at the crossroads which is the reason why it was and still is called Cage Lane.

Excessive intake of ale by some led to the erection of a cage giving the name to Cage Lane.

With the introduction of the Poor Law in 1572, most villages of any size had to provide food and shelter for the poor. Boxted's Poor House is thought to have stood on the north-east side of Workhouse Hill. It was probably demolished before 1838 when its site was Old Workhouse Yard.

An Act of Parliament of 1585 permitted Boxted men to weave cloth if they had been trading, or apprenticed to the trade for seven years, as they were known for the quality of their cloth and employed many poor people. Thirteen weavers were recorded between 1551 and 1670, 13 clothiers between 1583 and 1686.

Village constables were introduced and elected at the Annual Church Vestry Meeting. They, together with the Churchwardens and Surveyors, also elected at the Vestry Meeting, were responsible for the welfare of the Parish. All persons breaking the law had their misdeeds recorded. In 1600 John Sickerling, the parish constable, was ordered to arrest the putative father of the bastard child of one, Mary Andrews of Ardleigh. He refused. However, the man, Bradstrete, a servant at Rivers Hall was ordered to pay Mary the sum of eight pence a week until the child was seven years old and to deposit five pounds for the child's apprenticeship. Following the death of his employer, John Ive of Rivers Hall, he was left the sum of five pounds to reimburse him for the child's apprenticeship.

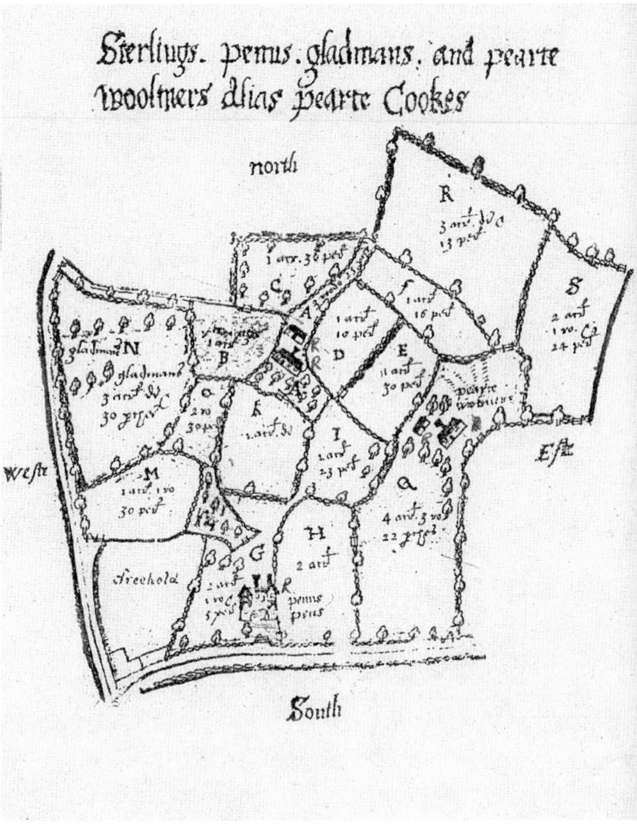

Map of Church Street showing Cleres and Gulsons, 1586.

The Great Migration

BETWEEN 1620 AND 1640 MANY PEOPLE LEFT England for The New World of America. Although economic considerations may have played a part in their decision, it seems that religious belief was the major reason for the exodus. The sailing of the Mayflower from Plymouth on September 6th 1620 carrying the Pilgrim Fathers to Massachusetts Bay marked the beginning of this exodus.

Towards the end of the reign of James I, when the Duke of Buckingham governed the country, any religious order outside the Church of England was discriminated against. When James died in 1625, and his son Charles came to the throne, matters did not improve. Charles' wife, the French princess Henrietta Maria was a devout Roman Catholic and held great influence over her husband. As a result the Puritan minority within the Church of England felt threatened,

It was inevitable that some of Boxted's inhabitants would take part in the Great Migration.

particularly in East Anglia where much of the wealth derived from the cloth trade belonged to these Puritans. Many parishes, Boxted among them, had a Protestant divine as incumbent, and the elders of the church the Maidstones were avid Puritans. It was inevitable that some of Boxted's inhabitants would take part in the Great Migration.

A few miles across the Suffolk border in the village of Groton lived John Winthrop who inherited Groton Manor from his father, Adam. John, with a group of like-minded men, looked overseas to America where they had visions of a new colony based on Puritan values. Together they formed the Massachusetts Bay Company with John Winthrop as governor. Plans were laid for a 'massive' migration to the colony, and the voyages that followed became known as The Great Migration. Eleven ships were prepared for this undertaking, and on April 6th 1630, five ships set sail from Yarmouth in the Isle of Wight with nearly 400 settlers on board. After a 10 week crossing they made landfall on a wild and desolate coast. The other six ships of the fleet sailed in May and arrived on various dates in July. Altogether the fleet brought about 700 settlers to Massachusetts Bay although it is thought that 200 people died during the crossing.

Sailing on the 'Arabella', the flagship of the fleet, were the Rev. George Phillips, vicar of Boxted, with his wife, Elizabeth and their three children, Samuel, Abigail and Elizabeth.

GEORGE PHILLIPS, b. Rainham, St. Martins, Norfolk, England 1593, d. Watertown, Mass 1 Jul 1644, m(1) a daughter of Richard Sargent, m(2) Elizabeth ____, (prob. the widow of Capt. Robert Weldon,) d. 27 Jun 1681

Reverend George Phillips, the first minister of Watertown, Massachusetts, was the son of Christopher Phillips of Rainham, Norfolk. He was born in 1593 at Rainham St. Martins, near Rougham, in the hundred or district of Gallow, county of Norfolk, England. George matriculated at Gonville and Caius College, Cambridge in April 1610 and graduated as a B.A. in 1613 and received an M.A. in 1617. 'He gave early indications of deep piety, uncommon talents, and love of learning, and at the University distinguished himself by his remarkable progress in learning, especially in theological studies for which he manifested an early partiality' (source of quote not provided).

George Phillips, the first minister of Watertown, Massachusetts, served for some years as vicar at Boxted.

He took orders in the Church of England and served as vicar at Boxted, Essex from 1612 to 1630, when he emigrated.

George Phillips was settled for a time in the ministry in the county of Suffolk, but suffering from the storm of persecution which then threatened the non-conformists of England, he determined to leave the mother country and take his lot with the Puritans. John Maidstone, a nephew of John Winthrop's second wife, was among George's parishioners (and later an officer in Cromwell's household). He wrote to Winthrop on November 4th 1629 stating that Phillips was resolved to go to Massachusetts and highly recommending him. He embarked for America

on April 12th 1630, in the 'Arabella', with his wife and two children, as fellow passengers with Governor Winthrop and Sir Richard Saltonstall, arriving at Salem on June 12th. Before the final embarkation which had been considerably delayed, Gov. Winthrop says in a letter to his son John Winthrop, 'From aboard the Arabella, riding before Yarmouth, April 5th, 1630. Yesterday we kept a fast aboard our ship, and in the Talbot. Mr. Phillips exercised with us the whole day, and gave very good content to all the company, as he doth in all his exercises, so as we have much cause to bless God for him'. George was one of the seven signees of The Humble Request, which is dated April 7th, prior to sailing, and which was printed that same year. There seems to be some ground for believing that George Phillips drafted this noble statement.

The Stour Valley looking towards Nayland from the great wood. (W. Barclay 2004).

George's wife died soon after arrival in Salem, and was buried by the side of Lady Arabella Johnson, both evidently being unable to endure the hardship and exposure of an exhausting ocean passage. He soon moved to Watertown, and without delay settled above the church in that place which was called together in July. At the Court of Assistants, August 23rd 1630, it was 'ordered that Mr. Phillips shall have allowed to him three hogsheads of meale, one hogshead of malte, four bushells of Indian corn, one bushel of oatmeale, halfe an hundred of salte fish'. Another statement from the same source says, 'Mr. Phillips hath 30 ac of land granted him opposite the Charles Ryver on the South side'. His first residence was burnt before the close of the year. His later house was 'opposite the ancient burial ground, back from the road'.

George continued to be the pastor of the Watertown church, greatly respected and beloved, until his death 14 years after his arrival. He died at the age of about 51 years, 1st Jul 1644 and was buried the following day. 'He was the earliest advocate of the Congregational order and discipline'. His views were for a long time regarded as novel, suspicious, and extreme, and he with his ruling elder, Mr. Richard Brown, stood almost unaided and alone until the arrival of Mr. John Cotton, in maintaining what was and still is, the Congregationalism of New England. 'It is not now easy to estimate the extent and importance of the influence of Mr. Phillips in giving form and character to the civil and ecclesiastical institutions of New England' (source of quote not provided). In 1632 George was one of the leaders in the protest made by Watertown against the action of the governor and assistants in arbitrarily levying a tax on the town. The tax was not remitted, but within three months an election of representatives to the General Court was agreed upon, with the understanding that in future no taxes should be levied without the consent of the court. To this Watertown protest, is rightly traced the beginning of representative government in Massachusetts. Accompanying the Phillips was the Stearn family whose daughter, Hannah, was the domestic servant to the Phillips family. In the 'Arabella's' manifest it shows that the Stearn family came from Stoke by Nayland, but records the Phillips as coming from Rainham, Norfolk. It was the place of birth that was recorded and not the place of domicile. A number of the emigrants settled in Watertown where George Phillips established a church. Other Boxted families to migrate at this time are thought to be the Pickerings, who settled in Cambridge, Massachusetts and the Bakers who established themselves in Charlestown. More people left Boxted in 1637 among whom were the Warners, Stones, Lumpkins and Bakers. It was thought they sailed on the 'Increase' but later research has disproved this and the name of their ship is unknown.

William Warner, a weaver, settled in Ipswich, Mass. in 1637, with his two sons, John and Daniel, and his daughter, Abigail. Where they lived in Boxted is in some doubt. The name given to their house was 'Merrylees Cottage' which is not traceable. It would appear that William's daughter, Abigail, was married. She had married Thomas Wells of Great Horkesley in 1634. Thomas left Boxted in 1635 on the 'Susan and Ellen'. It appears as though Abigail remained behind to nurse her mother who may have been sick, for she did not accompany the family to America. It is likely that she died prior to the rest of the family leaving for the New World. After his arrival in Massachusetts, Thomas Wells was granted five acres of meadowland in the name of his father-in-law William Warner, at Ipswich, Mass..

Bluebells have always put on a magnificent display in Boxted's woods. (W. Barclay 2004).

Another 1637 migrant from Boxted was Richard Lumpkin, a farmer, who lived at Parsonage Farm, Church Street. He was married to Sarah Baker at St. Peter's Church by George Phillips on October 20th 1614. Sarah and Richard settled in Ipswich, Mass. at the same time as William Warner. Relatives of Sarah (Baker) Lumpkin settled in Charlestown. Sarah was probably the younger sister of William Warner's wife which would account for the closeness between the Warners and Lumpkins. Accompanying the Lumpkins was William Bartholomew, a farm labourer, married to Ann Stone. Ann's brothers, Simon and Gregory Stone, had emigrated to Boston and Watertown from Great Bromley, Essex in 1635. The Stones were a Boxted family, all being born within the parish.

On arrival at Ipswich, Massachusetts, it would appear that William Warner received the following grant of land - 'One house lot, one acre more or less, in the Mill Street bounded on the east by another house lot as yet ungranted, (It was later occupied by Lumpkin), on the north-west by a highway leading from Mill Street to the High Street, butting upon Mill Street

The River Stour flows through the Dedham Vale between Boxted and Nayland on its way to the North Sea at Harwich.
(W. Barclay 2004).

at the south-west end, and at the north end, butting upon the swamp. Also a planting lot of six acres more or less, meadow and upland, and a farm of ninety and seven acres more or less, also a parcel of meadow, lying in the west meadows, being fourteen acres more or less.'

Little is known of William's life in Ipswich. He was known as a planter and was made a freeman of Ipswich on May 2nd 1638. There is also a record showing that he and William Bartholomew were appointed to lay out land granted to Richard Lumpkin and William Whittered. His family were spoken of as 'people of consideration'. William Warner died in 1648.

It is probable that Richard Lumpkin took the house lot next to the Warners and that he farmed the 97 acres of Warner's land. He died in 1642 and his widow, Sarah, married Simon Stone of Watertown in 1654. On November 10th 1654, Sarah Stone, née Baker ex Lumpkin, deeded to Daniel Warner, son of William Warner, her house lot and 158 acres of land in Ipswich. This underlines the relationship between Sarah and the Warners. Sarah went to live with Simon Stone in Watertown but they both returned to live in Ipswich. Thomas Wells, husband of Abigail Warner, became a freeman of Ipswich in 1637 where he died on October 26th 1666. Thomas deeded 340 acres of land and two house lots to his descendants.

It also appears that most of the other migrants from Boxted who had accompanied Rev. Phillips to Watertown found their way to Ipswich, together with those from Charlestown and Cambridge. There are records to show that the Stearn family, who left on the 'Arabella' in 1630, owned several house lots in Ipswich by 1650. These Boxtedians seem to have been very productive in their new land. Simon Stone had three wives and between them they produced 18 children. By the second generation the Warners had another 22 additions. It is said that 20% of the population of Ipswich, Massachusetts is descended from Boxted emigrants.

20% of the population of Ipswich, Massachusetts is descended from Boxted emigrants.

THE STUART PERIOD OF 1603 TO 1688 saw the struggle between King and Parliament for civil and religious liberty, the military dictatorship of Oliver Cromwell brought about by the failure to form a government by which the nation could be ruled by its elected representatives.

Boxted suffered during these times of struggle. The Church records were neglected between 1617 and 1644 and low morale led to many villagers emigrating to the North American colonies. A succession of non-conforming ministers created friction within the village. At the Quarter Sessions Elizabeth Nevard attested that she saw the vicar, Edmund Hickerigill strike John Maidstone in the churchyard while Nathanial Symonds said he saw John Maidstone urinating on men's heads from the loft of the belfry. In 1664 Edward Warner and Nathaniel Plumstead 'laid violent hands upon the vicar' when he refused to conduct the burial service of one, Ann Dymon, because 'she never went to church' and there was more trouble at a funeral when a child was thrown into an open grave.

> Matthew Hopkins, 'Witchfinder General', and his associates sent many innocent women to their deaths.

In the period following the first Civil War of 1645-48, 'witch fever' invaded the district. It was aided and abetted by extreme Puritanism and the bigoted preachers proclaiming this philosophy. Many innocent men and women thought to be Catholic, were denounced as witches and warlocks and hanged. Matthew Hopkins, a failed lawyer from Manningtree, set himself up as Witchfinder General. He and his associates sent many innocent women to their deaths - 19 condemned witches being hanged at Chelmsford on one day.

Boxted had its own witch, Elizabeth Potter, known locally as Betty Potter. She lived in a small cottage at one of the oldest gateways to the parish - Betty Potter's Dip. Legend has it that she cured the daughter of a wealthy Colchester merchant who, in gratitude, richly rewarded her. Her envious neighbours reported her to Hopkins as a likely witch. On hearing the accusation the merchant arranged her escape from Colchester, wandering the district for some time before settling in the cottage in the dip. Later she supposedly bewitched a team of horses pulling a waggon of wheat from Rivers Hall to the mill at Mile End demanding a sack of wheat to lift the spell. The event was reported to the Lord at Rivers Hall whose son organised a party to 'take the witch'. They seized Betty Potter and hanged her from a nearby tree. Matthew Hopkins was furious to hear of the hanging, as he was preparing to bring Betty to trial. He rode out with the

> They seized Betty Potter and hanged her from a nearby tree.

party of murderers to reclaim the body, only to see Betty Potter descend from the tree, cross the track and disappear - leaving behind only her clothes! Her ghost is said to appear at midnight on 21st October every year.

Boxted and The Civil War

Today, what was Boxted Heath is now farmland such as Old Farm.

THE GREAT CIVIL WAR BETWEEN KING and Parliament began on August 22nd 1642 when the King raised his Standard at Nottingham, and ended on January 30th 1649 with the execution of King Charles I. However from a military viewpoint the war consisted of two campaigns. Most of Essex was in favour of Parliament, resenting the high taxes levied by King Charles.

The First Civil War was from August 1642, and ended with the defeat of the King at Naseby in 1645. The Second Civil War began in the Spring of 1648, when a Scottish army came down to England to fight for the King. Cromwell defeated the Scottish force at Preston. At the same time, a force of 2,000 men of the 'Loyal Party' (supporters of the King), who had fled to France, landed in Kent. Commanded by Lord Goring and Lord Capel, who raised the King's Standard, many of the local gentry rallied to the call. They marched on London but were defeated at Maidstone by a Parliamentary army commanded by General Fairfax. The 'Loyalists' then crossed the Thames into Essex and marched north pursued by General Fairfax and his army.

On June 11th 1648 Lord Goring and the Royalist army arrived in Colchester and prepared to defend it.

Knowing that Colchester was a fortified town and also the home of one of their officers, Sir Charles Lucas, they decided to occupy Colchester and hold it until relieved by the Scots army which they considered would defeat Cromwell. On June 11th 1648, Lord Goring and the Royalist army arrived in Colchester and prepared to defend it. The Royalist force consisted of some 5,600 men of which 1,100 were horse (cavalry) and some 4,500 foot (infantry). The next day the Parliamentary forces arrived at Lexden.

During the first Civil War there was little activity in the Eastern Counties as they all supported Parliament - in fact the Earl of Essex was one of their commanders. It was during the 1648 resurgence in favour of the King that Boxted became involved in the conflict.

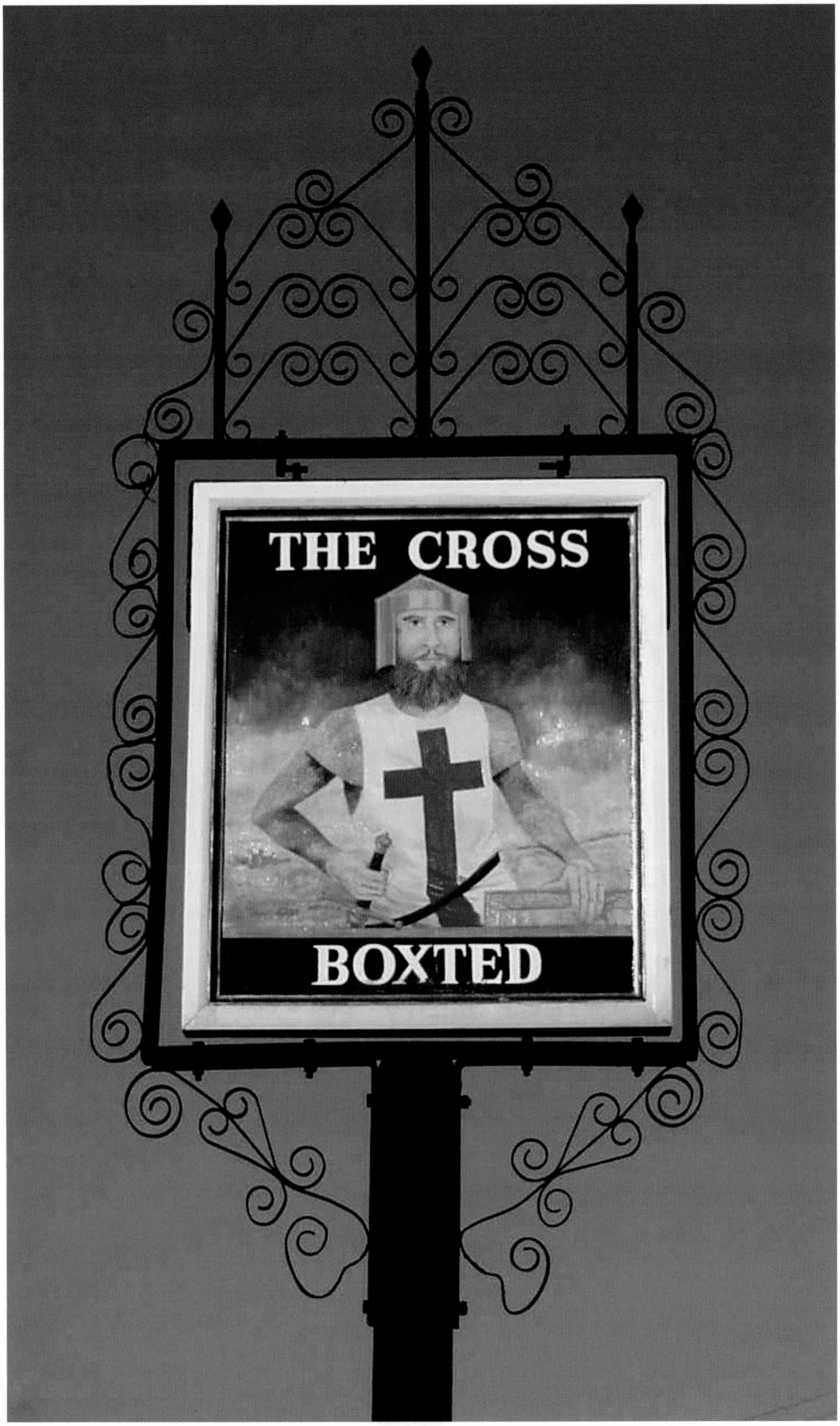
THE CROSS
BOXTED

The Boxted Covenant

THE FOLLOWING IS A TRANSCRIPT of the Covenant of July 1643 -

The vow and covenant appointed by the Lords and Commons assembled in Parliament to bee taken by every man in ye cityes of London, Westminster, the Suburbs and Libertyes thereof: And throughout the whole Kingdome was taken by the Inhabbitants of ye Parish of Boxstead, accordinge to ye order of Parliament.

I A.B. in humillity and reverence of the Devine Majesty declare my hearty sorrow for my own sins, and the sins of this Nation, which have deserved ye calamityes and Judgments that now lye upon it; And my true Intention is by Gods grace to endeavour ye amendment of my owne wayes; And that I do Abhorre and detest the said wicked and treacherous designe Lately Discovered; and that I never gave nor will give my Assent to the execution thereof, but will Accordinge to my power and vocation oppose and resist the same, and all other of the like nature; And in case any other like Design shall have after come to my knowledge, I will make such timely discovery as I shall conceive may best conduce to ye preventing thereof And whereas I do in my conscience beeleeve that the fforces Raysed by ye two Howses of Parliament, are Raysed and Continued for their just defence, and for ye defence of ye true Protestante Religion, and Libertyes of ye Subjects against ye fforces Raysed by the Kinge. I doe here in ye presence of Allmighty God, declare, vow and Covenant that I will accordinge to my power and vocation assist the fforces Raysed and Continued by both Howses of Parliament against ye fforces Raysed by ye Kinge without their consent: And will likewise assist all other persons that shall take this oath in what they shall doe in pursuance thereof: And will not directly or indirectly Adheare unto, nor shall willingly assist ye fforces Raysed by ye Kinge without ye consent of both Howses of Parliament. And this vow and Covenant I make in the presence of Allmighty God, the searcher of all Hearts, with a true Intention to performe the same as I shall answere it at the greate day, when the secrets of all Hearts shall be disclosed.

Signatures -

Nath: Kirkland Vicari - Robert Maydstone - John Barker - Robert Brooke - William Bradley - John Adkinson - John Messing - Randoll Willis - Samuell Warner - William How - John Maydstone - George Sheldrake - Henery Cressall - Richard How - Stephen Chamberlin - William Baker - George Burndish - William Downes - John Hawkins - Richard Johnsonn - Robert Eeles - William Cedick - Robert Lufkin - Tymothy Colsbur -Richard Colsbur - John Brane - George Ceole - Thomas Hone - John Sickerlin - William Sickerlin - Allen Hawkins - Thom ?? - Jonas How - Wilm Sharpe - Thom How - John Man - John Goodaild - Thomas Dawson - Daniell Adkinson - Robert Crowe - John Allin - John Webb - Richard Page - Richard Nevard - Thomas Lambe - Robert Baker - John Lawrence - John Southernwood - Daniell King - Robert Mixer - John Barker - William Barker - John Popse - John Bradleyes - William Jollye - John Rogers - Stehen ffisher - Thomas Kinge - Thomas Croyden - John Harden - Samerwell Adkinson - Roberte Hinsom - Edward Thurnwood Jnr - Joseph Perde - Stephen Downes - William Cunstable - Edward Ward - John Sheldracke - Robert Gibson - Thomas Stanfield - Thomas ?? - Thomas Harvey - Richard Lorance - Thomas Day - Samuell Browne - William Lorance - Edward How - George Pulham - Robert Diamond - Abraham Lufkin - William

Adkinson - John ?? - Jefor? Lowrans - Godfrey Larker? - George Moare - Edward warner - Edward ffurmswar?? - William Withersbe - Jeremia Applebie - Lionel Atkinson - John Burnebe - Richard Lafkin - John Apelbe - Thomas Cason - Willm Knap - John Bretton - Robte Welam elder - Robte Welam younger - Anthony ?? - Samuell Ward - John Hubbert - Edward Rancke - John Messing younger - Henrie Neverd - Thomas Dawson elder - Mychell Crowe - John Lines - William Constable - William Mixer - John Sherdricke younger - Stephen Sherdricke senior - John Angier - Robert Messinge - James Sheldrick - John Hospitt - Benjamin fferman - John Thurmmod - John Allen - ffraneces Kelcer - John Potter - Henry Mixer - Edward baker - Christopr Tinsley - Thomas Messing - Jonas Howe - Robert Greene - John Downes - Daniel Hinde - John Wynyef - Joseph Burnaebee.

Pray God yee all keepe it. (A total of 131 signatories)

THE OCCUPATION OF COLCHESTER by a Royalist army and the consequent siege of the town by Parliamentary forces set the scene for the involvement of Boxted in the war. This involvement stemmed from one of the attempted 'breakouts' by the Royalists.

EXTRACTS FROM THE DIARY (JULY 1648) of one of Sir Bernard Gascoigne's officers

"15th This evening all the Garrison Horse 1000 strong left by the Rye Gate and crossed the river at Middle Mill. (See Map 1). *We being at the head of the column and some 30 minutes in advance, we being in strength four troops* (200 men) *proceeded to the west of Fothergill's Encampment. Our pioneers laid down the hedges and embankments, and we passed Fothergill's Encampment without disturbing the enemy. When we passed into Boxted at some 20 minutes past midnight we heard the sound of battle behind us and knew the enemy had been alerted. Sir Bernard decided to advance to*

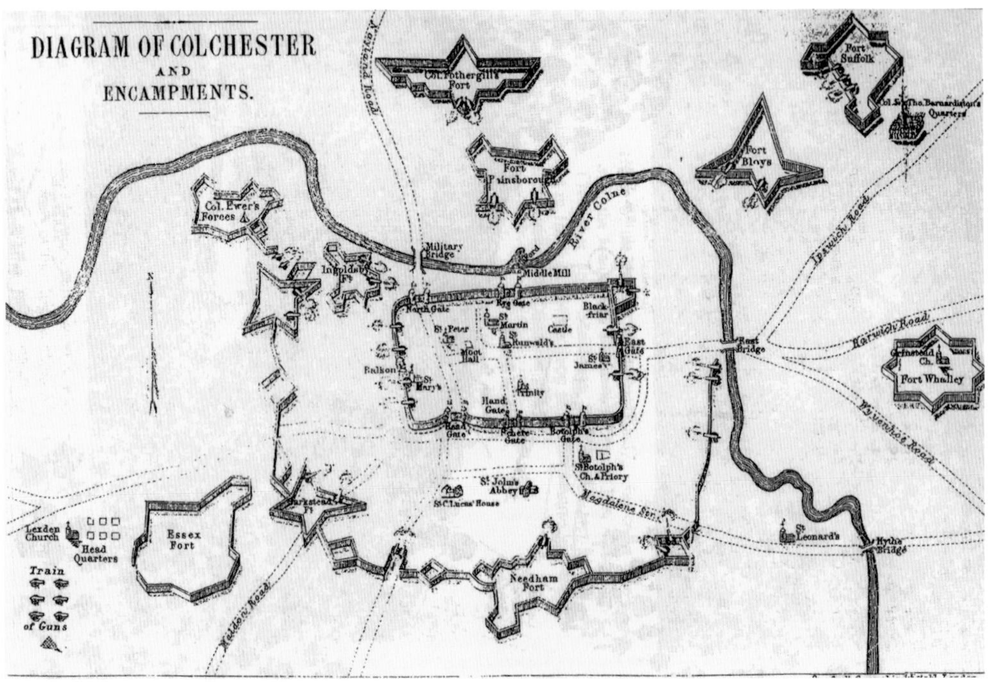

Map 1: The encampment at Colchester 1648.

Boxted Heath where there was some cover, and to wait for the rest of our force.

16th. As dawn broke and the rest of our horse had not arrived, Sir Bernard dispatched riders to look to the country towards the Causeway (Nayland Road now A134). *They returned mid-morning to report Local Trained Bands of muskets and pikes were defending all approaches. Sir Bernard, looking at his charts,* (See Map 2) *considered that if we returned toward the woodland for cover, and then, leading our horses, came up upon their flank, we could overpower them and hold the pass to the Causeway till help arrived. This we did, and as we fell upon them they threw away their weapons and fled.*

17th. We continue to hold our position, Sir Charles Lucas and Sir George Lisle have not arrived and we consider they have been forced to return to the town. Sir Bernard decides we must do the same, and we send forward our baggage. As we prepare to retire, a large force of enemy horse are seen preparing to attack us. We take position, and with Sir Bernard at our head, we charge, breaking the enemy line. However, we are very much outnumbered, and, leaving many of or dead and wounded on the field we abandoned our baggage, and disperse, and make our own way back as best we can. Those of us fortunate enough to get back, will reform and enter Colchester by the East gate where we still hold some of the outer works.

18th. Some two troops of our number (100 men) bedraggled and weary enter the East gate of the the town to find that Sir George Lucas and Sir George Lisle have suffered the same fate as ourselves, and like us, are very dispirited."

Four days later on July 22nd, Sir Bernard Gascoigne and his remaining horse escaped from Colchester via the Maldon road following a fierce engagement with the enemy and passed toward Tiptree Heath. Having good guides they escaped to Cambridgeshire where they dispersed. Sir Bernard Gascoigne was never taken. Following the abortive attempt to escape via Boxted, a troop of Roundhead horse were stationed at one of the large houses in Boxted Church Street.

Postscript

There are many stories and events and happenings during the period of the siege of Colchester which concern the village. One of these tells of the escape from Colchester of Lord Goring, the Royalist commander. Although this diary of events cannot be substantiated by study of the official history of the siege, a local discovery tends to lend credence to the story.

One very wet night in early July 1648, a party of Royalists dressed in the uniform of the Parliamentary Army escorted a covered wagon, in which was a very sick Lord Goring, out of the North gate of Colchester. The Roundheads had at this time not completed their encirclement of the North of the town, relying on the river to deter any attempt by the Royalists to escape. There was a military bridge across the river and this was guarded by Fairfax's men. On the night in question, the Roundhead sentry seeing a number of men in Parliamentary uniform with a covered wagon approaching the bridge, made no attempt to stop them and allowed them to cross.

The Royalist party proceeded North across Mile End Heath to Boxted, then over Boxted Heath to the Cross Inn. The landlord being in sympathy with the Royalist cause agreed for Lord Goring to stay at the Inn for a day or two while arrangements were made to get him out of the country. Two days later Lord Goring was taken to Langham, where he was rowed up the river to Manningtree to join a ship for France.

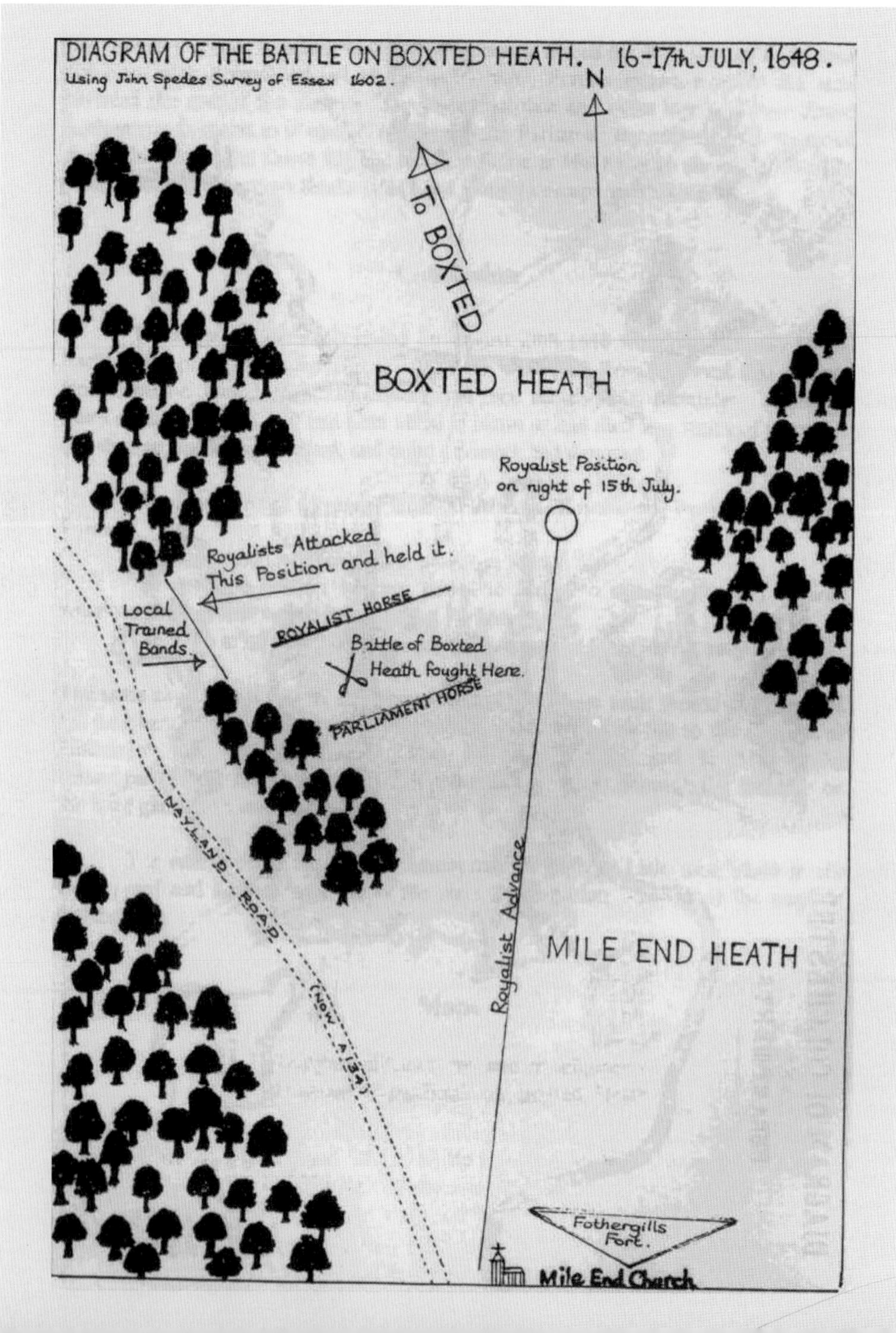

Map 2: The battle of Boxted Heath.

Meantime his Loyal supporters remained in the vicinity of the Cross Inn to cover his departure. Unfortunately the Roundheads discovered what had happened, and that members of their Army billeted near Boxted Cross were really Cavaliers in Parliament disguise. A Roundhead force was dispatched from its Colchester encampment, the Royalists were set upon, and many of the Loyal Party were killed, still wearing their Parliamentary uniform.

In 1925 when renovations to Hillhouse Farm (near Boxted Cross) were being carried out by Messrs. Deaves of Nayland, it was noted that a plaster wall seemed not as solid as it should have been. When the wall was removed it exposed a small powder room (of 18th Century origin - used by gentry to powder their wigs). In the ceiling of this room a trapdoor was seen and when a workman forced the door the skull of a man complete with

Roundhead helmet fell upon him. Further examination of the attic revealed the rest of the skeleton plus breastplate and other items of Roundhead equipment. It seems as if one of the Royalists in Parliamentary uniform was wounded in the skirmish at the Cross Inn and hid in the attic of Hillhouse Farm to die of his wounds. This tale does support the story of Lord Goring's escape via Boxted.

The skull of a man complete with Roundhead helmet fell upon a workman renovating Hillhouse Farm.

Conclusion

THE SIEGE OF COLCHESTER ENDED ON AUGUST 28TH 1648 with the surrender to the Parliament Forces of the Royalist garrison. Of the 5,600 Royalist force that entered Colchester on June 11th, 3,526 officers and men remained to surrender. Although many of the missing 2,100 had been killed in battle or had died as a result of poor diet and disease, some had escaped, and quite a number had deserted.

The conditions of surrender imposed upon the Royalists by Parliament were as follows:
The Lords and Gentlemen all prisoners of mercy. The common soldiers to have passes to return to their homes, but without weapons, and on oath not to serve against Parliament. The town to be preserved from pillage, paying £14,000 ready money.

Hillhouse Farm where the skeleton of an unfortunate Royalist was found in 1925. He had hidden in the attic to escape the bitter siege of Colchester only to die of his wounds.

The same day General Fairfax called a council of war about what should be done with the prisoners of war. It was resolved that the Lords should be left to the disposal of Parliament; also that Sir Charles Lucas, Sir George Lisle, and Sir Marmaduke Gascoigne (brother to Sir Bernard) should be 'shot to death' although the sentence on the third gentleman was respited. The execution of Sir Charles Lucas and Sir George Lisle took place in the Castle yard and a monument marks the place of execution. So ended the siege of Colchester.

The execution of Sir Charles Lucas and Sir George Lisle took place in the Castle yard.

Mention has already been made of the burden of high taxation levied by the King. In 1635 a 'pontage' tax was imposed. This taxed the movement, by road, of corn, straw, hay, timber, firewood, clay, sand, bricks, tiles and all household goods, effectively raising the cost of all these commodities transported to Colchester. To avoid the tax on the transport of wheat a post mill was built on the edge of the heath at Mill Corner, where the miller's house still stands. Unfortunately the end of the Civil War saw further tax increases to maintain Cromwell's Model Army and his military campaigns in Ireland. With the Restoration in 1660 everyone expected better times, but it was not to be.

In 1665-66 a new strain of bubonic plague decimated the village. The records of the parishes of Colchester indicate that nearly 50% of the town's population perished in this epidemic. In 1674 a Hearth Tax on each household was introduced, but in Boxted 53% of the households were judged to be too poor to be taxed with a further 10% unrecorded for taxation, being paupers.

William III to George III 1688 - 1820

As the 18th century dawned, Boxted, like so many other villages, stood on the threshold of change. The wool trade that had brought so much prosperity to the village in the 15th Century had gone into rapid decline. Although many people were still employed as weavers, the wool had to be imported from other parts of the country and the Enclosure Acts of the late 18th and early 19th Centuries had a disastrous effect on the rural poor. The common lands where they had grazed their animals and grown food for their families were 'enclosed' and either formed new farms or were added to existing farms. Boxted Heath was enclosed in 1815. Eventually the proper rotational system of cropping became established, and yields from arable land began to rise.

At this time we begin to see the naming of fields, names that are still in existence in the Boxted of today. Intriguing names such as Pipeingwent Grove, Witchfield, Trooper's Pond field, Boat field, Sawpit field and Lynefield lay alongside fields, recalling old tenants, owners or a special feature. For example, White Arch for Whiteacres, Perryman for Pannymers, Hallberries probably derives from Aubreys (Aubrey de Vere, Earl of Oxford, owned Boxted Hall) while Shoulder of Mutton field describes its shape.

Boxted Heath occupied most of the south of the parish in 1777. In the early 19th Century it provided over 30 farms with sheep and cattle pasture, furze and turf, and clay to repair the cottages. The Heath was enclosed in 1815 and was highly cultivated by 1848. Small farms at this time cultivated wheat, barley, rye, clover and trefoil with turnips being grown in the fallow years. There were three grocers' shops within the parish in 1754, and again in 1778, and two butchers in 1780. With the increasing prosperity of agriculture came the establishment of the servicing trades. Horses outnumbered the human population, so the farriers and blacksmiths were the first to arrive, followed by the wheelwright, harness maker and saddler. The smithy, situated in the Street not far from the Cross Inn, lay next door to the Wheelwright, while the saddler worked from premises round the corner in Cage Lane. One landlord of the Inn was also a butcher who opened a shop in a thatched barn next to the Inn in 1790. There were already two millers in the village, and in 1800, a bakery was established in the Street close to the blacksmith.

The village charities benefited from bequests during this period. We already had the Thomas Love charity, and in 1732, a Mr Norman gave some property near the east gate of the church for the 'benefit of poor widows'. These cottages later became the almshouses to be administered by the churchwardens. Robert Gilder left property on the edge of Boxted Heath in what is now Lords Lane, to the parish. The estate consisted of a parcel of land called Lynefield, two cottages and a small wood. In his will he stipulated that the income from the property should be used for the benefit of the poor widows of the parish. The cottages and wood were sold at the beginning of the 19th Century and the land, afterwards known as the Widows field, was sold in 1956, the money being invested for the purpose intended by Robert Gilder. Another benefactor gave land near the church called Camping Close to be a place of recreation. The village school was built on this land in the 19th Century. The parish was also endowed with two

A pair of Devon oxen at Parsonage Farm in about 1890 harnessed to a gallows plough.

gravel pits - one near Betty Potter's Dip and the other, Holloway, was near Runkyn's Corner.

Many houses in the village were rebuilt or improved at this time. Rivers Hall was completely rebuilt in 1715 and some additions were made to Boxted Hall. Cheshunts was extended and improved. In 1762 the village acquired its second public house a beerhouse in Mill Road named the Greyhound. The existing village inn was now given the name of the Dog and Partridge which, in the 1850s, became known as The Cross after the landlord, John Cross. Unfortunately the health of the village did not improve during the 18th Century. Smallpox replaced bubonic

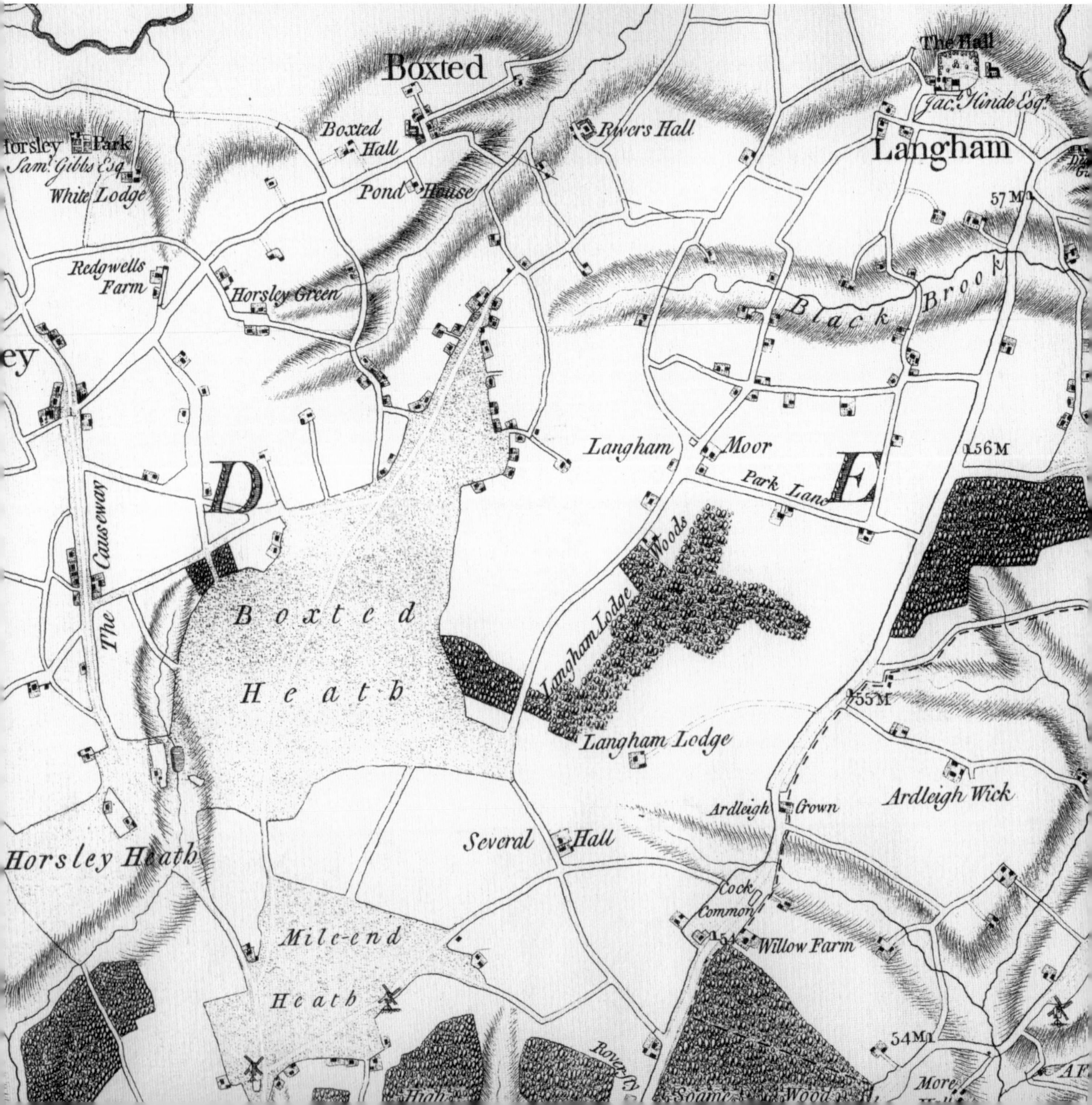

Map of Boxted 1777.

plague with local epidemics in 1730, 1737 and 1798.

Boxted was an unruly place in Georgian times. The village fair which was held on the heath where Eastside now stands generated considerable disorder. This fair, which lasted several days, encouraged large numbers of people not only to stay all day but a large part of the night as well. Unlawful games were played, heavy drinking and other debaucheries encouraged, which led to an increase of vice and immorality until, in 1761, an order was made for the suppression of unlicensed fairs in Boxted and other villages.

Horses outnumbered the human population so the farriers and blacksmiths were the first to arrive.

George IV, William IV and Victoria 1820 -1901

THE NAPOLEONIC WARS LEFT THE COUNTRY SHORT of most commodities especially food. These shortages gave a welcome boost to agricultural prosperity - in fact the price of wheat recorded in 1819 would not be equalled for 120 years, at the start of yet another war.

The Blacksmith's photographed in 1907 for an auction sale by Fenn's.

Boxted shared in this prosperity, and with the enclosure of Boxted Heath in 1813, many more acres were brought into production. The Heath was subdivided into a geometric pattern of fields which were sold at auction. To gain access to the fields, roads were laid out dividing the main areas of fields into blocks. Boxted Straight Road was extended from the house called Heath (now Holly) Cottage to Betty Potter's Dip. Other roads leading off Straight Road included Chapel Road, Mill Road, Queen's Head Road, Langham Road and Ivy Lodge Road. Ellis Road was also constructed at this time. These roads were surfaced with stone. At the auction of the heathland John Freeman of Rivers Hall and William Beaumaurice Rush of Boxted Hall bought most of the land. Other large purchasers were William Fisher and John Joscelyn.

Boxted was an unruly place in Georgian times.

Machines began to appear on the agricultural scene with steam traction engines being developed and harnessed to many farming operations. Threshing was now done entirely by machine, while specially modified steam engines were used for ploughing and cultivation. Steam engines were placed at either end of a field and pulled eight furrow ploughs across the field by means of wire hawsers.

Boxted Lodge, the home of William Fisher Hobbs, renowned 19th Century farmer (1920).

At this time one of the country's leading farmers and cattle breeders lived and farmed in Boxted. He was William Fisher Hobbs whose portrait hangs in the Farmers Club in London (page 144). He lived in Boxted Lodge, a fine 19th Century house originally of two storeys, now three. He also owned and farmed Enfield's farm. Many stories tell of his quest for farming excellence and the good relations he had with his workforce. On one occasion he sent 20 men with weeding hooks to walk through his wheat and barley to remove any thistles. Returning to the farm late in the day they reported that they had done what he had asked of them. Fisher Hobbs asked how many thistles they had found. "Five, Sir" was the reply. "Well," said Fisher Hobbs "You will have to go back again tomorrow for there are two more thistles to be cut."

In 1825 Thomas Cudden sold the windmill on Mill Corner by auction. He wished to sell the property because of his poor health. The lot consisted of a post Windmill with two pairs of French stones, a round house complete, sash-fronted brick-built dwelling house with garden, an oven for six bushels, stable cart lodge, piggery and pump with excellent water. It was sold at the Waggon and Horses on North Hill, Colchester for £425. The new owner, Henry Sparkes, improved the mill, and with the village enjoying 'good times' success was assured. However, by 1855 the mill stopped milling flour, producing a small amount of animal feed for a few more years before falling in disrepair. It was demolished towards the end of the Century.

During the first half of the century, Boxted's population grew with the expansion of agriculture. White's Directory for 1848 gives the population as 856, which by 1863 had risen to 935. The

Directory of that year lists the following activities:

25 farmers; six publicans; two millers; six shopkeepers; two wheelwrights; one baker; one blacksmith; one harness maker; three shoemakers; five academies of learning; one butcher and a Post Office complete with person to deliver the letters. There were eight paupers.

Steam engines were placed at either end of a field and pulled eight furrow ploughs across the field by means of wire hawsers.

Cheap imports of wheat and barley from North America had their effect on British farming and the supporting industries, and White's Directory of 1873 tells a different tale - 12 farmers; five publicans; one miller; one shopkeeper; one wheelwright; one baker; one blacksmith; one harness maker; no shoemakers; one private school; one butcher and a Post Office. Unemployment in the village is recorded as 140 persons and 15 paupers.

The owners did not always occupy the two manors and the lands were rented out to local farmers. Several large houses were built in Boxted between 1805 and 1860. As well as Boxted Lodge previously mentioned, Priory Farmhouse on Boxted Straight Road and Boxted House in Church Street were built at this time.

Steam threshing at the turn of the 20th Century.

The Victorian era saw a great improvement in law and order. During his time at the Home Office between 1822 and 1830, Sir Robert Peel drastically reduced the number of capital offences although the law remained harsh for many trivial offences. In 1863 at the Essex Assize in Chelmsford the 29 year old William Wooton was sentenced to four years penal servitude for stealing 58 postage stamps.

The five tailoresses and four dressmakers recorded in 1851 were

At the end of the century we note many village names whose descendants still live in Boxted today.

probably outworkers for Colchester clothing companies. Ten years later these figures had increased to 16 tailoresses, four dressmakers and three needleworkers.

In 1894 Boxted's first Parish Council was elected, taking over the duties of the Parish Vestry. 14 parishioners stood for election and over 100 village residents attended the election. Capt. H. Eley became chairman with Robert Maylyn as the Parish Clerk. Other successful candidates were Lt. Col. A.H. Lefroy, Mr E. Knight, Mr G. Page, Mr W. Baxter, Mr R. Sweetlove, and Mr W. Scragg. Capt. Eley lived at Boxted Hall, Lt. Col. Lefroy at Boxted Lodge while Mr Sweetlove farmed Old House Farm, and later, Barritts. Later notable parishioners included Mr Henry Munson; the renowned carpenter and carriage builder, Mr Charles Dennis who lived at Redthornes and Mr W. Bird, the landlord of the Cross Inn.

Boxted House (K. Barclay 2004).

The Post Office, Straight Road.

At the end of the century we note many village names whose descendants still live in Boxted today. Mr J. Welham, the wheelwright and carriage builder, lived at Great Blakes. The blacksmith was a Mr Cooper who was followed by Bert Turner; Jim Munson, landlord of the Butcher's Arms, was the village carrier. Johnny Cole was the baker and the Postmaster, Josiah Biggs also baked bread which he delivered on his bicycle with the letters.

The Post Office sold groceries, together with Misses Smith and Vesey's shop near Windmill Close. Groceries were also sold at Robert Maylyn's shop, at the junction of Straight Road and Queen's Head Road, and Billy Baxter's shop in the end of what is now Ash House at the top of Workhouse Hill also sold groceries. Tobacco and confectionery were also available in the six pubs which doubled as shops. The village had two butchers - the licensee of the Cross, Mr W. Bird, and Mr W. Page in Straight Road.

The Cross Inn (1920).

The Village shop.

The Twentieth Century

THE 1901 CENSUS SHOWED BOXTED to have a population of 680 - a far cry from the great agricultural year of 1863 when the village was home to 935 villagers. Many had left the village to work in Colchester and other towns but fortunes were about to change. Farming began to prosper again, and in 1908 the Salvation Army began building houses on their smallholding estate on Straight Road. The scheme was initiated in 1906 when a Mr Herring loaned the Salvation Army a sum of money to establish a labour colony to put 'landless people on people-less land'. Priory and Old House farms were bought together with some previously copyhold land on Straight Road, Horkesley Road and Accommodation Road. Semi-detached houses were built with five acres of land part of which was planted to fruit. Many Londoners from the East end settled into the new smallholdings. Only a nominal rent was charged in the first year, whilst implements and seed were provided free of charge. After two years the tenants were expected to have made the smallholding pay, but many of the new tenants had no experience of working the land and their situation after two years was probably worse than when they arrived in Boxted.

In July 1910, General Booth, with many eminent dignitaries and politicians lunched in a marquee on the estate and visited some of the 67 smallholdings of between four and seven acres of which about 50 were occupied. When the procession of carriages carrying the party was passing the site in Mile End where the new Mental Hospital was being built, General Booth halted the procession and addressed the company from his carriage on the evils of drink, which, in his opinion, led to the necessity to build mental hospitals.

The Queen's Head, which was situated close to the smallholdings, was seen by the Army as a threat to the sobriety of their tenants so most Sunday meetings were held in the road outside the pub assuring the landlord and his customers of their damnation to the fires of Hell if they did not repent and give up strong drink. On Monday morning many of the attending tenants would be seen at the back door of the pub filling their jugs with best ale.

Within a year of General Booth's visit discontent had risen to a dangerous level. The produce of the smallholdings was gathered in a large building, Priory Hall, near Priory House, which was used part as a citadel and part as a packhouse. The produce was graded and packed before being taken to Colchester for sale. Some of the produce was not sold and that which was, often returned unrealistic prices. After the eviction of several tenants, the Charity Commission held an inquiry at the Moot Hall in Colchester. The inquiry cleared the Salvation Army of maladministration but the evictions continued with much publicity. The Salvation Army scheme was wound up in 1916 and the smallholdings were bought at auction, together with Red House Farm, Enfields Farm and Ivy Lodge Farm, by Essex County Council. The houses were used to resettle servicemen returning from the Great War. Some of the tenants bought their properties on 999 year leases.

In 1905 there were fifty farmers in Boxted.

In 1905 there were 50 farmers in Boxted, 36 holding less than 50 acres of land. The 2,500 acres of arable land was sown to clover (789 acres), wheat (376 acres), oats (322 acres), barley (280 acres) and mangel-wurzel (110 acres). There were also 65 acres of peas, 61 acres of potatoes, 51 acres of beans and smaller plots of rye, cabbages, kohlrabi, vetches or tares and lucerne. The large acreage of clover together with over 400 acres of grassland supported 373 cattle, 810 sheep and 287 pigs. There were 79 acres of coppice and 14 acres of orchard.

Priory Hall off Straight Road was also bought by the County Council and became the Village Hall for many years. During the Second World War it was home to a flourishing social club and a venue in the area for 'Saturday night hops'.

Lt. Col. Lefroy of Boxted Lodge, did not farm the attached land but let it out to H. & E. Edwards who established a market garden. The improved rail service from Colchester to London meant it was possible to send the produce to the London markets. Mr A.W. Sexton later converted Plains and Barritts farms to market gardening before buying the land used by Messrs Edwards who had moved to Ardleigh.

Plains Farm 1908.

Village Businesses

Another successful market gardener was Mr Sydney Whiteman of Noaks Farm. Among the smallholders, successful market growers were Charles Nichols of Garden Cottages, George Clarke of 51, Straight Road, Harold Larman of 61, Straight Road and Mr E. Whitnell of Peppers Lane. Mr Whitnell's wife, Hannah, was a Boxted character of the '20s and '30s who delivered fruit and vegetables in Boxted and Mile End in her donkey cart.

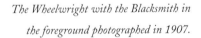

Mrs Hannah Whitnall with her fruit and vegetable delivery donkey cart.

Mr A.W. Warner established rose cultivation at 25, Straight Road but the business has now gone and the land returned to arable.

In 1901 the telegraph office opened in Boxted Post Office in Straight Road next to Speeds house. Josiah Biggs ran the Post Office with a flourishing grocery business and bakery. The bakehouse lay behind the post office. The bakery died with Mr Biggs but the post office continued for many years under the direction of Mrs Mabel Garwood.

The bakery in the Street prospered under Mr 'Johnny' Cole who made bread deliveries to the surrounding villages. His son, Charlie Cole, took over the business which he ran until his retirement after the Second World War. Curiously, another Charles Cole who had owned a London bakery before coming to Boxted succeeded Charlie.

Kelly's directory for 1902 records two butchers in Boxted. Mr W. Bird had a butcher's shop and slaughter house next to the Cross inn, and Mr Walter Page had a shop in Straight Road opposite the site now occupied by the British Legion hall. Another butcher in Church Street is recorded in 1906 but there is no reference to a shop. This may have been a Mr George Whipps who had no premises but sold meat from his cart. No record can be found when the Cross

The Wheelwright with the Blacksmith in the foreground photographed in 1907.

Mr Lewis Welham, painter. (1910).

butchers closed but Mr Bird left the Cross just before the First World War. Mr Walter Page's shop closed just after the war when Mr Cecil Green opened a butchery business in Straight Road beside Randall's (Smith and Vesey's) shop. A slaughterhouse was built at the rear of the premises. Mr Green was Boxted's butcher for many years before he retired and sold the business to Mr O. Thorpe of Langham.

Smith and Vesey's shop in Straight Road next to Windmill Close changed hands just before the 1914-18 war when a Mr Randall bought the property. Something of an entrepreneur, Mr Randall started a radio business in the very early days of the 'wireless' when they were powered by batteries. Everyone went to 'Randalls' for their batteries and to have their accumulators charged. Mr Randall later started a garage business and installed a petrol pump. When Mr Randall left Boxted, Stanley Hales bought the shop and Denis Geater, the garage business. Mr Hales ran the shop for many years retiring in 1961 when the rise of supermarkets forced its closure.

Mr Geater built up a thriving haulage business which was nationalised after 1945.

Mr Geater expanded the garage and built up a thriving haulage business which was nationalised after 1945. He restarted the business after denationalisation and was succeeded by his son. The business is now closed and the site is now the Windmill Close development.

Maylyn's shop on Straight Road near Queen's Head corner closed before the 1914-18 war but 'Billy Baxter's' shop in the end room of Ash House continued under several proprietors until it moved across the road to a bungalow. It closed in 1930.

The prosperity of the wheelwright and blacksmith was linked to the heavy horses used on the farms, and as they were gradually supplanted by machines, the work of the two trades diminished. Both businesses closed after the Second World War. John Welham, the wheelwright in 1901, was followed in the business by his sons, Lewis and Alan Welham. Mr Banham was blacksmith and farrier in 1906 and he was followed by one of Boxted's

The Wheelwright's Yard.

Fire damage at St Ives Farm, September 4th 1919.

most popular characters, Bert Turner, who was Boxted's last 'smith'.

For many years the only transport to and from Colchester was by Munson's cart. Mr Jim Munson was the landlord of the Butcher's Arms. Every Monday, Wednesday and Saturday he would carry people and goods to Colchester. He also collected bundles of tailoring from the homes in Boxted to be delivered to the clothing factories in Colchester returning with new work for the seamstresses. Mr Munson closed the carrier business when the Butcher's Arms was closed in 1919.

In the early 1920s Mr Clifford Went set up a bus service from Boxted. In the early days Clifford would use his vehicle to transport livestock to Colchester market on Saturdays. He would then return to Boxted, clean out the vehicle and use it as a bus to take the villagers into town. Eventually he established a very successful bus service but, unfortunately, Mr Went died in early middle age. His widow, Alice, continued the business and expanded it from premises in Mill Road before retiring and handing the business over to her son, 'Dod' Went. On his retirement, the company was bought by Hedingham Coaches who operate the service today.

The Two World Wars

THE FIRST INDICATIONS OF POSSIBLE WAR came to Boxted in 1911 when a military exercise was held in the area. The schoolchildren were allowed out of school to watch the soldiers and their horses muster in Church Street. Recruiting sergeants visited the Boxted beer houses to persuade the young men to 'take the King's shilling'. Many of Boxted's young men had already joined Lord Haldane's newly-created Territorial Army while others had signed on with the Essex Yeomanry. In this regiment one had to provide one's own horse. All these young men reported for duty when war was declared in 1914 and some were sent to France. More men volunteered for 'Kitchener's Army' before conscription was introduced in 1916. Eventually men up to the age of 50 were called up for military service leaving the women and elderly men to maintain village life. Horses were compulsorily bought from the farms and hay was in short supply.

Men from the Norfolk regiment were billeted in the unoccupied houses on the heath before being posted to the Dardanelles where many were to die. Sixteen Boxted men lost their lives in the First World War.

Memorial in St Peter's Church to those of the parish who fought and died in the great war; 1914 -18.
(L. Douglas-Menzies 2003).

World War II

BOXTED'S CIVIL DEFENCE PRECAUTIONS had gas masks issued to the village population in 1938 following the German invasion of Czechoslovakia. The ARP wardens were based in a room in Mill House on the corner of Mill Road which also acted as a first aid post. The local Auxiliary Fire Service (AFS) mounted nightly watches from the school.

Children from the Carpenter Road school in East London were evacuated to Boxted together with the teaching staff. Mr Tom Pissarro reported to the Parish Council that 93 children, nine

One hundred high explosive and numerous incendiary bombs fell on Great Horkesley, Boxted and Langham.

teachers and 15 mothers with children had been successfully accommodated in the village. Priory Hall was used during the day as a schoolhouse for these evacuees. Once the German invasion had reached the French coast the East of England had become the 'front line', and most of the evacuees were moved from Boxted and taken west of London.

Boxted's first experience of enemy action came on July 15th 1940, when a lone Dornier 17 bomber strafed Mill Road with machine gun fire, but there were no casualties. The aircraft flew on to drop eight bombs on West Bergholt, five of which failed to explode. On August 16th German aircraft jettisoned their bomb loads on their run home, dropping 100 high explosive and numerous incendiary bombs on Great Horkesley, Boxted and Langham. Once again most of them failed to explode. Little damage was done and there were no casualties.

On Saturday February 20th 1944, a single German raider dropped a stick of bombs which caused more damage and casualties than any previous enemy action. Two houses at the corner of Perryman's Lane were destroyed and three cottages close to the Cross Inn were burnt out. Forty other properties suffered minor damage. Nine of the injured were taken to hospital but they all recovered. The air-raid warden Tom Alderton was highly praised for his efforts in rescuing eight people from the demolished homes.

In April 1944, a badly-damaged Liberator bomber of the US 8th Air Force was circling over the village. The crew baled out leaving the aircraft to crash in open fields near Kerseys in Church Road. Later that year Boxted witnessed its first V1 flying bomb. It fell in a field where Eastside housing estate now stands. A thatched cottage was set on fire, but quickly put out. Two more flying bombs landed in Langham without causing much damage.

The crew baled out leaving the aircraft to crash in open fields near Kerseys in Church Road.

On Sunday, September 17th 1944, the local Royal Observer Corps counted 1500 aircraft and gliders flying over Boxted on their way to Holland. The armada took 1½ hours to pass over the village.

Many Women's Land Army girls were billeted at Gulsons while working on Boxted's farms.

Boxted House was used as the headquarters for anti-aircraft units in the area. A searchlight unit was stationed at Noakes farm off Straight Road.

Many of those too old or too young for service in the armed forces volunteered for the Local Defence Force (LDV), which became the Home Guard. Boxted Home Guard formed 'C' company of the 8th battalion with headquarters in Colchester. Major Waller was commanding officer of the Boxted Home Guard before being promoted to command the 8th battalion as colonel. Other members of 'C' company were Lt. F.Bradford and Lt. D.Geater who was later promoted to Captain. The Home Guard was stood down in November 1944.

'C'company Boxted Home Guard.

Left - Right

1. Back Row	J.Minter	T.Graves	J.Clarke	P.King	F.Cooper	B.Keen	C.Cole	J.Tayliss	A.Nicholls	H.Spurgeon	
2.	R.Scott	B.Sollis	R.Hirons	T.Taylor	W.Peck	R.Farrant	- Tabakoff?	R.Newell	L.Whitehouse	- Cook	- Squirrel	T.Walke
3.	H.Schofield	A.Smith	H.Whitnell	J.Cummins	R.Fletcher	- Thorpe	- McLaughlan	C.Minter	F.Gardiner	F.Gardiner	- Harvey
4. Front Row	B.King	T.Atkins	H.Gant	H.Scott	F.Bradford	Col. Waller	D.Geater	F.Warner	J.Bacon	A.Brewer	C.Green

A Martin Marauder takes off, watched by a farm labourer (believed to be Bill Sparkes) and two young boys whose bicycles can just be seen on the left in the foreground.

Boxted Airfield

THE MOST IMPORTANT U.S. FIGHTER BASE IN THE U.K.

Although named Boxted, the airfield is alongside Park Road in Langham. The reason for the anomaly is that there was already an airfield named 'Langham' in Norfolk.

Boxted was allocated to the American 8th Airforce in August 1942. Built by French & Sons, a construction company from Ipswich, using both Irish and local labour, it was constructed to the standard American bomber base plan designed to accommodate B17 Flying Fortresses, but the first group to arrive flew the Martin Marauder.

Lester Maitland: first Commanding Officer of Boxted airfield. He was the first man to fly an aircraft over 200 MPH; the first to fly from the U.S. mainland to Hawaii. He became an Episcopal priest after the war. He died on March 29th, 1990 aged 91.

Most of the photographs of the airfield have been kindly supplied by Richard Turner, Boxted Airfield Group.

The 386th Medium Bomb Group arrived on June 10th, 1943. Their commanding officer was Lester Maitland, a famous aviator. He was one of the two pilots to make the first flight across the Pacific. The 386th missions were mainly bombing of enemy airfields.

Boxted airfield bombed

On the night of August 17th 1943, Boxted was attacked. Two men were killed and 29 injured.

Fitting auxiliary fuel tanks beneath the wings of a P51 Mustang.

Mustang Group

The next unit did not arrive until November 1943. This was the 354th Fighter Group known as The Pioneer Group because they were the first to fly the new Merlin-engined P51 Mustang fighter. When fitted with additional drop fuel tanks they could escort bombers all the way to Germany. They were led on their early missions by Lt. Col. Don Blakeslee - one of the few American fighter pilots who had combat experience.

Over the next weeks, after the original C.O. Kenneth Martin became a P.O.W., Major James Howard took command and they quickly established the Mustang as an outstanding aircraft.

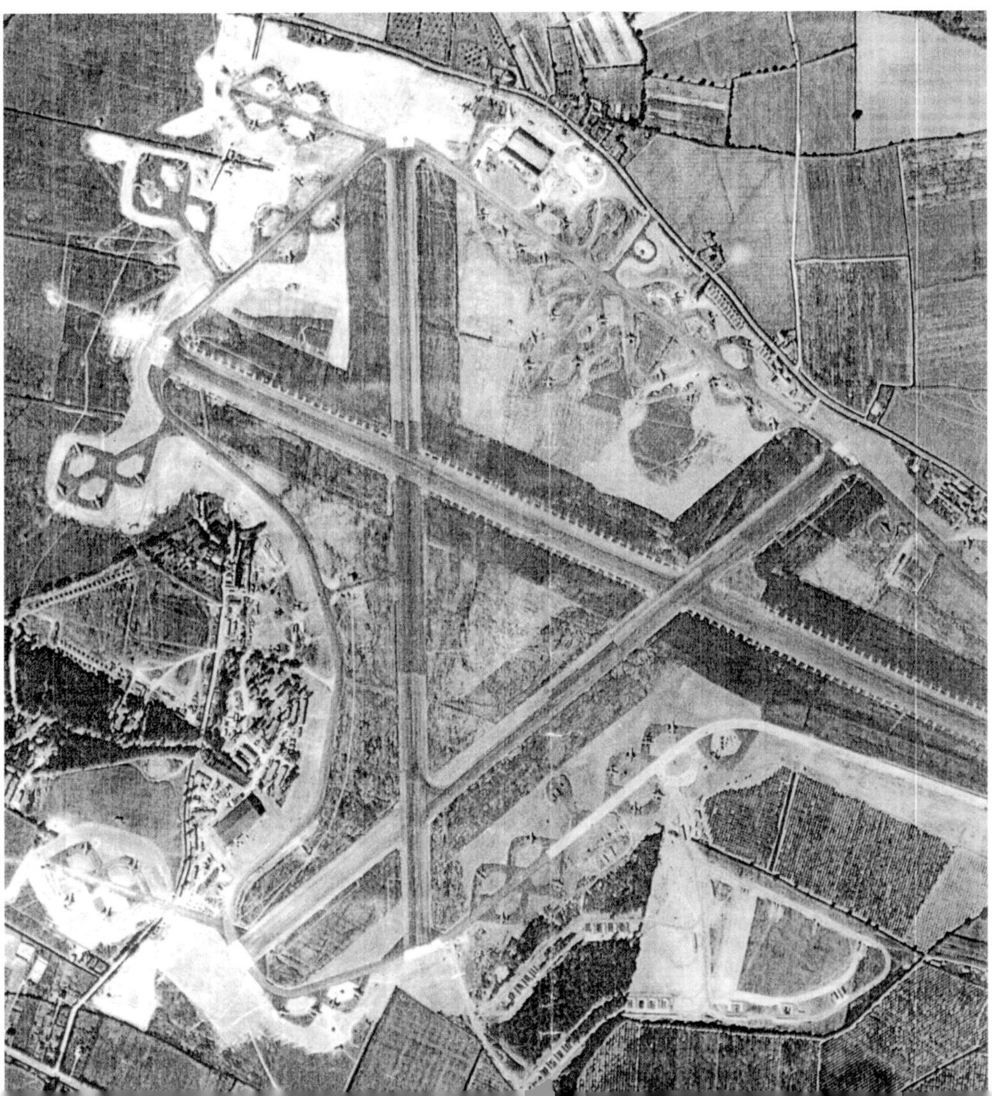

Boxted airfield: a 1943 German reconnaissance photograph. One can see Marauders parked around the apron.

Major Jim Howard in his Mustang P51B. Painted on the side is evidence of his ability as a fighter pilot both in the Far East and at Boxted.

Howard went into the attack and single-handedly fought off about 30 Me110's for about 30 minutes.

On one mission, Howard, suddenly finding himself alone, sighted a formation of Luftwaffe fighters attacking the 401st Bomb Group. Howard went into the attack and single-handedly fought off about 30 Me110's for about 30 minutes. He destroyed three and damaged several others. It was a brilliant performance for which he was awarded America's highest award for bravery, the Congressional Medal of Honor. Having proved themselves and their aircraft an outstanding unit, the 354th left for Lashenden in Kent to prepare for D-day.

The Wolfpack

The next group to arrive were one of the most famous in the US Airforce, the 56th Fighter Group, known as the Wolfpack. They were led by Col. Hubert Zemke. He was a tireless and determined commander who would not accept second best from his men. The Group flying the P47 Thunderbolt included some of the best pilots - Gabreski, Schilling, Rankin, Johnson and Comstock. The Group had more 'aces' (five positive victories in the air) than any other group.

A P47 Thunderbolt: Hairless Joe on the nose of the aircraft marked it as Dave Schilling's. The eve of D-day (June 5th 1944) 'invasion stripes', five alternate white and black 18 inches wide were applied to wings, and around the rear of the fuselage 18 inches forward of the tail plane, this was to identify allied aircraft.

The Polish Flight

Gabby Gabreski became the highest scoring 'ace' in the highest scoring fighter group in the entire 8th Air Force during World War II with a total of 28 'kills'. Gabreski had started to train as a doctor before he enlisted, in 1941. Stationed at Wheeler Field, Hawaii, he was there when the Japanese attacked Pearl Harbour. Despite getting airborne during the attack he was unable to destroy any enemy aircraft. With his fluent Polish, he eventually joined the 315 Polish Squadron flying the Mark IX Spitfires out of Northolt. Various postings took him to Kings Cliffe in Northants' Horsham St. Faith (now Norwich airport) where he was given command of the 61st Fighter Squadron and then to Halesworth where he scored his first victory over the Luftwaffe. By the time he arrived at Boxted on April 18th 1944, he had accumulated 18 confirmed 'kills'.

'Polish flight' of the 61st F. Squadron. Left to right: Boleslaw, Mike Gladych, Tadeusz Sawicz, 'Gabby' Gabreski, Zbigniew Janicki, Tadeusz Andersz and Witold Lanowski.

Early September 1944 Air Sea Rescue Squadron CO's aircraft, 5F-A 'Tony' on a dispersal loop at the back of Moor Farm, now Dove House. (Note the WW on the tail denoting 'War Weary'.) Beyond the hangar are cottages in Park Lane.

On a visit to Northolt to meet his Polish friends he found that most of the action was taking place beyond the range of the 315 Squadron Spitfires and the Poles were becoming disillusioned. The P47 with two additional fuel tanks could reach 500 miles from base. After talking with Col. 'Hub' Zemke it it was agreed to transfer the six Polish pilots to the 56th Fighter Group at Boxted - Zbigniew Janicki, Tadeusz Sawicz, Tadeusz Andersz and Kasmierz Ritkowski. These were later joined by Boleslaw, Gladych and Witold Lanowski. Of these six Poles, Janicki was killed in action.

He flew too low and struck the ground with his propeller.

A curious fact about the Poles in the 56th Fighter Group is that the RAF refused to pay them while they were with the USAAF, and neither could the Americans. To overcome this the other pilots of the 56th had a collection for them every pay day. On July 5th 1944 Gabreski made his

28th and final kill before he was due to return to the States on leave and to get married. On July 20th he could not resist the temptation to take part in one last mission to attack the Luftwaffe airfield at Bassenheim. On his second strafing pass he flew too low and struck the ground with his propeller. In spite of this he managed to make a forced landing in a nearby field. After five days on the run he was captured and passed the remainder of the war as a POW. The Group moved to Little Walden in October 1944.

The 386th Bomb Group were considered the best of the American Medium Bombardment groups of WWII.

Gabreski died of a heart attack in January 2002, aged 83, and was buried with full military honours in Calverton National Cemetery, New York.

The RAF took over at the end of the war and used the airfield until 1947 with various squadrons of Mosquitos and Meteor jets. The airfield was used for some private flying until the mid-1960s.

Law and Order

BOXTED PROVED TO BE A VERY LAW-ABIDING village in the 20th Century. Misdemeanours were mostly of a trivial nature such as riding a bicycle without a light, trespassing with intent, poaching, drunk in charge of a horse, and incapable while sitting in the road! The resident constable lived next door to the old Post Office in the house called Speeds.

However, Boxted did make headlines in 1919 when one Edward Halls was accused of setting fire to Speeds Farm, The Street, Boxted, and home of William Page. The house and barns were

Firemen assess the fire damage to Speeds Farm.

destroyed together with some fowls, sheep and a pig to the value of £800. The defendant, who had been employed by Mr Page, had been sacked for his drinking habits. Found guilty on the evidence of Sgt. Bird and Sidney Cason, vermin catcher, he was committed to Chelmsford gaol for three years.

In 1912 there were harrowing descriptions on the local press of evictions of the smallholders by the police who had to force their way past the barricades. Between the wars there were reports of beggars in the Street and thefts of fruit, and of one farmer watering his milk.

Family under eviction 1912.

Boxted's murder occurred on January 6th 1958, when Leslie Peck, a local tractor driver, found the body of a young girl in a ditch beside the Dedham Road. She had been brutally beaten; some of the 17 wounds to her head fracturing her skull and others breaking bones in her hands as she attempted to defend herself. The victim proved to be 19 year old Mary Kriek, a Dutch au pair girl who worked at Bulbanks Farm at Stanway outside Colchester. She had come to England to be near her sister Willi, who worked as a mother's help at a neighbouring farm in Eight Ash Green, Colchester. In spite of exhaustive searches and door-to-door enquiries in Boxted, Stanway, Eight Ash Green and Holland, no one was ever apprehended for the crime.

Health and Doctors

FROM 1912 LOCAL DOCTORS HAVE HELD SURGERIES IN THE VILLAGE. The first surgery was held in Maylyn's schoolhouse by Dr Slade of Nayland. The schoolhouse was converted to a bungalow and occupied by a Mr and Mrs Thorpe where Dr Helm of Great

Horkesley conducted surgeries. The surgery later moved to 54 Straight Road and again to 59 Straight Road. Dr Slade retired in 1939, and Dr Cran took over his practice. Dr Helm was called up for National Service in 1939 and Dr Cran held the Boxted surgeries during the war years. Dr Helm retired after the war to be replaced by Dr R. Berry who built a surgery with a waiting room as part of a bungalow on Mill Corner. Following Dr Berry's retirement, surgeries by a group practice, were held in the Village Hall.

Weather

Boxted is very fortunate to have continuous local weather records since 1902. In 1903 between June 13th and 16th there were 60 hours of continuous rain totalling almost five inches. This is still a record for the South of England. Following this deluge there was no rain at all for the next three weeks so that the corn and hay harvests were disasters.

Wet harvest 1912.

Boxted had heavy snowfalls and white Christmasses in both 1908 and 1909. On April 19th 1909 a heavy snowstorm left snow six inches deep. 1911 was the hottest summer on record. In June there were seven consecutive days when the temperature reached 95°F and, the 20th, topped 101°F. Summer rainfall that year was two and a half inches and the total yearly rainfall was 20 inches.

Sixty hours of continuous rain totalling almost five inches. A record for the south of England.

Sunday April 27th 1919 saw a great snowstorm, followed the next day by rain and thaw. This resulted in extensive flooding when the road under the Colchester North Station bridge was flooded three feet deep.

1921 was the driest year on record with no measurable rain from March to September. The total rainfall for that year was just under 10 inches. The following year was the exact opposite, with rain or snow being recorded on 205 days of the year. On June 29th 1927 an air frost destroyed the bean and potato crops. 1933 was another very dry year with just 11½ ins of rain being recorded. This drought inspired the Parish Council to clear out the village pond, but resolved that in the next year 'no further water supply is required in the parish as it would entail a rate and payment for use'. Five years later mains water was available to most of Boxted. The village had to wait until 1975 before a mains drainage system was installed. Even now, in the 21st Century, many houses rely upon cesspits and septic tanks for waste disposal.

The hurricane of 1987 struck the village in the early hours of Thursday, October 16th.

1947 was another severe winter followed by a hot summer. From the February 11th to 15th the temperature did not rise above freezing, day or night. On February 13th, 27 degrees of frost was recorded while on July 9th the temperature reached 97°F.

1962 was a much colder winter than 1947 but with less snow with the lowest night time temperature falling to -5°F, 37 degrees of frost. The average afternoon temperature of February 1963 was 31°F. It was the coldest winter since 1740.

1987 saw the arrival of the hurricane which struck the village in the early hours of Thursday, October 16th. At 4.50am a wind gust of 100mph was recorded. Many trees fell, tiles blown from roofs and portable buildings destroyed. Power and telephone lines were brought down leaving the village without power or communication for four days.

The walnut orchard at Boxted Hall Farm after the 1987 hurricane. 70% of the English walnut trees planted by Carter & Blewitt were lost.

The Long Barn, Rivers Hall Farm. Sections of both ends were destroyed (see page80).

CHAPTER TWO

SAINT Peter's Church

St. Peter's Church, approached from the East gate.

Building and Dedication

ST. PETER'S CHURCH WAS BUILT on a ridge of land to the South of the River Stour. Christian Saxons started the building just before the Norman Conquest, using rubble and Roman bricks for a simple structure, and thatch for the roof. When the Normans came they completely rebuilt the Church, employing the same Saxon labourers, and the Norman masons who had built Colchester Castle.

St. Peter's Church was completed sometime between 1090 and 1130.

This early church, consisting of the tower, nave and chancel, was completed sometime between 1090 and 1130; the North and South aisles and porch being

Left: The south porch of St. Peter's. (R. Thompson 2004).

GARDINER AND MEARS - BELL FOUNDERS

Thomas Gardiner had a long and prosperous career. He worked in Sudbury for several years from 1709, starting a foundry at the same time as John Thornton, another local founder. He then moved to Bracondale foundry near Norwich from 1745 to 1758 and returned to Sudbury where he died in 1762. There is documentary evidence that he was also casting at Ingatestone, Essex in 1739. However, Gardiner bells are found in abundance all over the eastern counties, as he cast over 250 bells from 1709 to 1760.

Thomas Mears junior of the Whitechapel Foundry started casting in 1810, the example at Chiddingly being one of his earliest bells. He cast the bell for St John's Hospital, Winchester, in 1825. In his earlier years he used the title 'T. Mears'. By this time he had almost a complete monopoly of founding, and continued to purchase local foundries, moving their business to London. He died in 1842.

Very little is known about the Sudbury foundries, but there is evidence of two sites, and they seem to be quite independent of each other. The Bury Post contains information which indicates that they were sited at 'the Hospitallers Yard, near Ballingdon Bridge and, successively, Curds or Silkweaver's Lane'.

added much later. The Tower used rounded stones, mortar, old Roman Brick and iron puddingstone.

Robert of Horkesley and his wife, Beatrice, remarkable philanthropists of their day, helped to establish St. Peter's Church having already founded a Cluniac Priory at Little Horkesley. The monks, a branch of the Benedictine order from Cluny in Burgundy, were seconded from the monastery at Thetford. In support of the monks, Robert and Beatrice gave half the income from Boxted church, and their demesne in Boxted.

The first priest recorded at Boxted church was a monk called Roberto.

In 1140, one of these monks, Roberto, became the first priest recorded at Boxted church. He lodged with Robert and Beatrice at their house that stood where Pond House is today, until a small Priest Hut was built on the North side of the church.

The original church was dedicated to St. Mary, and was changed to St. Peter after the Reformation.

The Tower

THE TOWER OF ST. PETER'S IS considered to be one of the best Norman square towers. The Norman masons based its construction on a small castle keep, and some of the earliest timbers still found in the tower are probably Saxon.

The upper part of the tower collapsed in the 16th Century, and was rebuilt with irregular English-bonded red brick, and a third storey and buttresses were added.

Opposite: Church East end and Albery Cottages photographed in 1913.

In medieval times, it is believed that the tower contained four bells. Three bells were recorded in 1684, and again in 1845, but only two in 1909, one of which was cast by Thomas Gardiner of Sudbury, Suffolk, in 1714, and the other by Thomas Mears of London, in 1812. The 1714 bell was used as the bidding bell until 1999. Unfortunately it is no longer safe to ring either bell. Legend has it that the third bell was sold to settle outstanding parish bills.

The Church Tower and West Wall. (L. Douglas-Menzies 2003).

The Nave and Aisles

A REPORT BY THE COUNCIL FOR BRITISH ARCHAEOLOGY 1977, describes how, when the roof was raised and the two small windows were built above the chancel arch, the arch was left intact. It describes the nave roof as four bays long, supported by three king posts with moulded plates and tie beams. Although much obscured by plasterwork it is nevertheless a handsome example.

The Nave, Chancel and central aisle. The photograph shows the magnificent Norman chancel arch with 'plain impost (the capital of a pillar which receives an arch) and plain roll moulding'. (L. Douglas-Menzies 2003).

The North and South aisles were added in the 14th Century, and the Report mentions the fact that the arches on the South side are much higher than those on the North side. This difference in height and their plain state, without the formations of imposts or the use of any stone dressing gives the nave an unusual appearance.

The wall plaster is largely ancient and there is every possibility that it covers earlier wall paintings.

St. Peter's Church ca. 1920.

To build the aisles, the Norman round-headed windows were blocked, and the nave walls were opened up to form steeply pointed arches. The outline of the Norman round-headed windows on the nave walls and the Norman roofline can still be seen.

In the early days the church would have had an earth floor and no seating for the congregation. The old and infirm would have stood against the nave walls for support while the young and fit stood in the middle, hence the origin of the saying 'weakest to the wall'.

In the 16th Century the roof was re-thatched, and in 1604 a domestic style dormer window was introduced above the South clerestory. Later a niche - possibly for an icon - was carved in the wall below the chancel arch. The thatch was removed from the nave roof in the 18th Century, and replaced by tiles. At the same time the North door was blocked and replaced by a window.

The old and infirm would have stood against the nave walls for support... hence the origin of the saying 'weakest to the wall'.

After the Reformation it became compulsory to display the Royal Arms. The Royal Arms bearing the Hanoverian escutcheon are found on the North wall of the nave.

Kingposts in the roof.
(L. Douglas-Menzies 2003).

Set into the aisle floor are two memorial slabs, one to Alexander Carr (died 1681) and one to John Marr (died 1683), both servants to the Earl of Oxford. The Earls of Oxford, - the de Vere family - were the owners of Boxted Hall at the end of the 17th Century, and Anne Bayning, later Anne de Vere, was resident at the Hall.

Choir Stalls along the south wall. (L. Douglas-Menzies 2003).

There are other memorial tablets set into the floor of the nave commemorating Rev. Robinson, his wife and son, Charles.

In 1870 the architect Mr A. W. Bloomfield, a son of the Bishop of London, extended the North aisle to form a vestry. He also re-seated the nave and was responsible for the Victorian pews.

The Font

RESEARCH SO FAR HAS FOUND little history of the font. The carving of the lock and rose suggests late 17th or early 18th Century. However the stem is more characteristic of a 19th Century reproduction - probably the result of the 1836 Grant from the Incorporated Society for the Enlargement of Churches and Chapels. The Incorporated Church Building Society (ICBS) was founded in 1818 and incorporated by Act of Parliament 10 years later. Its purpose was to 'remedy the deficiencies of places set aside for Public Worship in our towns and cities'.

The font has been restored to its original place inside the South door having been moved during Bloomfield's restoration in 1870.

The font was moved back to just inside the south door in 2005 when a new floor was laid throughout the nave.

The Chancel and Sanctuary

LITTLE IS KNOWN OF THE ORIGINAL Norman Chancel, as it was completely rebuilt in the 16th Century, when the tracery windows on the

CLAYTON & BELL

RICHARD CLAYTON (1827 - 1913). Coming from the North Country, Richard Clayton spent times at Leigh's Art School and the Royal Academy School of Sculpture. One of his first stained glass commissions was in St Nicholas' Church, Brighton in 1848.

ALFRED BELL (1832 - 1895), came from Stilton on the borders of Wiltshire and Dorset. As a 15 year old he travelled to London and found a place in Gilbert Scott's Studio in 1847. CLAYTON & BELL set up their business together around 1854. Their first work was a series of windows for the Nave Clerestory at Westminster Abbey in 1856, (destroyed in the Blitz of World War II). Commissions followed in Rochester Cathedral and Sherbourne Abbey.

Whilst they undertook other forms of church decoration and furnishings, they were artists first and foremost, using stained glass as their preferred medium. Business flourished and by the end of the 1860s they had 300 employees on their books, who painted backgrounds and grisaille, draperies, folds, texts, inscriptions, etc. Their immense West Window can be seen at King's College, Cambridge, and the Great East Window at Bath Abbey.

"They want a decent surplice for their minister."

sidewalls were installed. Part of the old windows remain above the tracery windows, and in one of these are fragments of ruby and blue glass, probably 14th Century, which escaped destruction by Parliamentary soldiers during the Civil War. Even their long pikes were unable to reach the highest decorations of churches, hence it is often the highest windows that escaped the Puritan pillage.

By 1633 the chancel had fallen into disrepair - the church guardians, Richard Burndiche and Ranulphus Willis, reported that "Their Church wants tyling and glazing, the chancel ceiling wants repairing. They want a decent surplice for their Minister. A new pulpitt with a rober, a new communion table and a decent carpet of broadcloth or silk for the server".

In 1705, cracks in the East and South windows needed repair; the walls needed plastering and the whole chancel whitening. This damage could have been the result of the Great Storm of 1703.

In 1870, Messrs. A.W. Bloomfield re-seated and re-floored the chancel. The memorial floor slabs to the Maidstones and Sir Richard and Lady Blackmore were re-sited in the sanctuary. During this restoration a heating system was installed, and the boiler was placed in the 12th

Century Priest Hut, which was unfortunately demolished during a later modernisation.

At this time, the stained glass window was added. It was a gift to the church from the Norman family as a memorial to their father, Rev. Charles Norman, vicar of the parish 1832 - 1867.

The window was created by Messrs. Clayton & Bell of London, who were responsible for many excellent Victorian and Edwardian stained glass windows in Britain.

In 1935 the chancel floor was re-paved, and the parishioners erected the clergy and choir stalls to mark the Silver Jubilee of King George V.

Rev. George Murton donated the reredos in 1924 in memory of his wife. It was designed by the architect W.H.R. Blacking, whose work can be seen in Gloucester and Chichester cathedrals. It was painted by W. Gales of the Victoria and Albert museum, who was also Secretary to the Church Advisory Committee.

The Chancel ceiling was decorated with a celestial design in 1999.

The clear glass windows allow a flood of light to enhance the rich texture of the chancel. In 1999, Messrs. Howell and Bellion of Saffron Walden decorated the chancel ceiling with a star motif on a dark blue background which reflects the strong colouring of the East window and reredos. At the same time the chancel was painted and the reredos restored.

Opposite: East end tracery windows which were installed in the 16th Century.

In addition to the floor slabs in the sanctuary in memory of the Maidstones and Sir Richard

Blackmore's poetry was much admired by Dr. Samuel Johnson.

Blackmore, the chancel contains several more memorials. On the North side there is a further memorial to Sir Richard Blackmore and his wife. Sir Richard, who lived at Pond House, was physician to King William III and Queen Anne. He wrote many books on theology and medicine whilst his poetry was much admired by Dr. Samuel Johnson. On the South wall there is a small epitaph to Elizabeth Maidstone, wife of Nathaniel Bacon. Elizabeth was the daughter of John Maidstone of Pond House, who later moved to Boxted Hall.

Other memorials are wall tablets to John Joscelyn of Boxted Hall and Rev. George Murton.

Looking west up to the gallery and organ. (L. Douglas-Menzies 2003).

The Gallery and Organ

St. Peter's is one of the few churches retaining a Western gallery. William Fisher presented this gallery, which houses the organ and choir, to the church in 1836. In the same year the church received a grant from the Incorporated Society for the Enlargement of Churches and Chapels. The grant provided a further 125 seats. There were now 120 free seats where previously there had been 74.

About 1875, an unknown benefactor presented to the church a single manual organ built by Henry Jones. This organ is unique and was probably commissioned for a private chapel.

The gallery is supported at the front by four metal pillars, and seats about 25 people. Access to the gallery is obtained by a wooden staircase from the base of the tower. Beneath the gallery are form seats that are very likely to have been found in the church before Bloomfield installed the pews in the nave in 1870.

The pews have brass cardholders for reservation by the hierarchy of the parish. The central pews were reserved for the gentry at the front, followed by landowners and

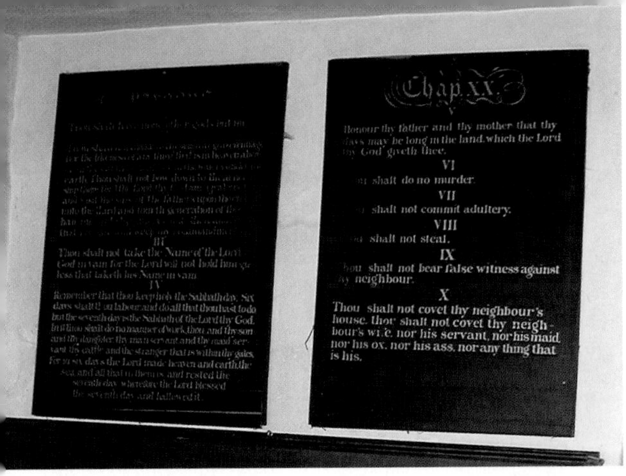

The Ten Commandments (L. Douglas-Menzies 2003).

farmers. The aisle pews seated the small business people - farm managers, head horsemen, wheelwrights and farriers. Labourers used the seats beneath the gallery which were not 'reserved', but they were probably pleased to have any seat at all, having been caused to stand in previous times. Victorian wall plaques beneath the gallery depict the Ten Commandments, while the board over the tower door records the restoration of the tower by the Blewitt family in memory of relatives who lost their lives in the Second World War.

The South Porch

THE FINE, LARGE SOUTH PORCH probably dates to the late 16th Century, and retains some of the original oak timbers. It was altered in the 17th and 18th Centuries and restored in modern times. The walls are mainly large flints while the corners are modern coping stones. The Victorian lamp, formerly oil, is now electric.

The South Porch. (L. Douglas-Menzies 2003).

The Pulpit and lectern. (L. Douglas-Menzies 2003).

The Pulpit and Lectern

THE MARBLE PULPIT is an exceptional addition to the church. It could be said that it is out of keeping with a mediaeval church, but since St. Peter's had no previous pulpit, it serves as a dramatic Victorian improvement.

The husband and family of Marianna Freeman Corton who died in 1881 erected the pulpit in her memory. She was the daughter

Memorial to Ann Maidstone 1692.

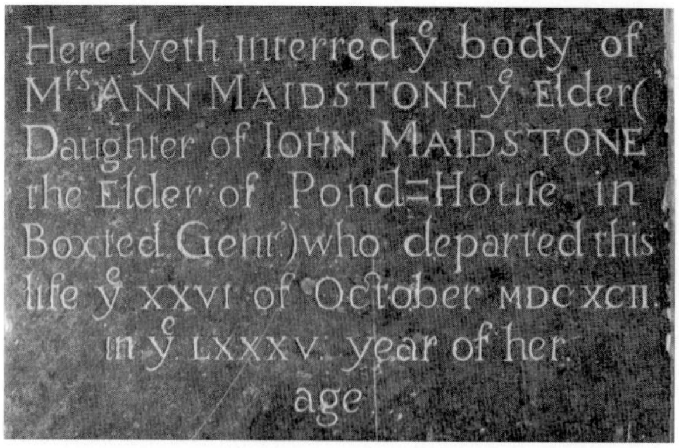

of William Freeman, a descendant of John Freeman, who owned Rivers Hall and a large amount of land around Boxted. The Freemans were indirectly related to the de Vere family, Earls of Oxford.

The lectern was presented to the church by descendants of the Rev. George Phillips, vicar of the church from 1615 until 1630. Rev. Phillips emigrated to Massachusetts in 1630, and established the church at Watertown on the Charles River.

Memorials

THE FLOOR TABLET IN THE SANCTUARY to Ann Maidstone is one of three in memory of the Maidstone family. The family resided in Boxted for nearly 100 years, living at both Pond House and Boxted Hall. The Maidstones were strict Puritans and friends of Oliver Cromwell. John Maidstone, Snr., the father of Anne, was a member of the Commonwealth Parliament.

People still remember 'Miss Lefroy' bicycling round the village in a voluminous skirt and black bonnet.

The Vesey Mausoleum

The Vesey mausoleum.

ON THE SOUTH SIDE OF THE CHURCH stands an unusual granite and marble mausoleum built in 1890 containing the remains of Arthur Sidney Vesey, Captain in the Norfolk Regiment militia, and Hon. Major in the Essex Regiment militia. He died of pneumonia following a riding accident in 1890, aged 35. Also within the building is a second coffin, thought to be that of his wife.

The coats of arms and motto over the door match exactly those of the Roscommon Veseys. It seems possible that Vesey's father was a steward for the Lefroys. The Lefroys were an Irish family from Longford who bought Boxted Lodge and its land from the Fisher Hobbs family. The Lefroys and Veseys would, as landed gentry, have known each other before moving to

Memorial to John Grimwood

Boxted in the mid-19th Century, as Roscommon and Longford are adjacent.

Lt. Col. Hugh Augustin Lefroy's daughter lived at Perrymans on the Dedham Road, Boxted. Known locally as 'Miss Lefroy', people still remember her bicycling round the village in a voluminous skirt and black bonnet. She died in 1951.

Arthur Vesey, in the Essex Regimental records, is described as a farmer. His widow probably moved to The Elms (known as Scarletts) next to the church after his death. She is said to have gone to the mausoleum every day to read to her deceased husband. There is a hanging lantern of unusual design within the mausoleum which gives some credence to the story.

There are further memorials in the vestry. One is to John Grimwood, Barrister-at-Law, and for many years Recorder of Colchester, and another to Ann Cooke, widow of Rev. Robert Cooke, vicar of Boxted, 1753 -68.

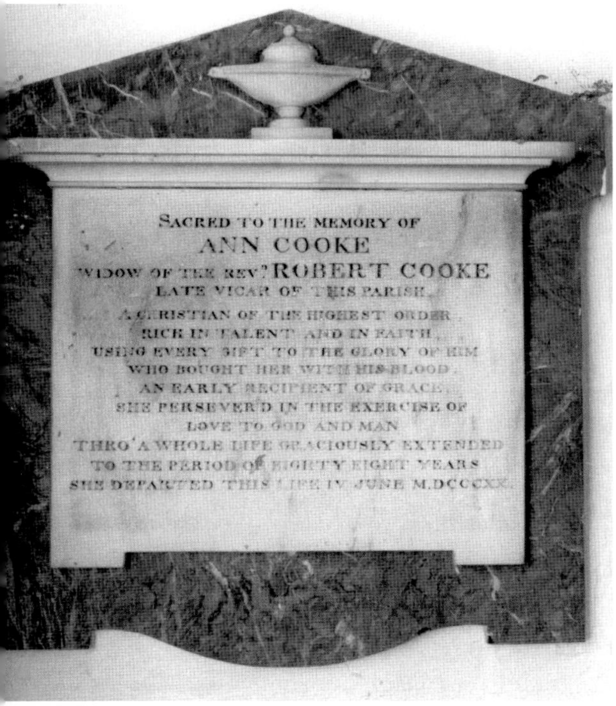

Memorial to Ann Cooke.

On the wall of the South aisle are two memorials to the Fallen of the parish who lost their lives in the two World Wars.

Priest Hut

It is thought that the early priests, who were monks from Little Horkesley Priory, were housed in a hut on the North side of the church. From 1140 until 1332, almost 200 years, there are no records of incumbents at St. Peter's. Although from 1185 the moieties were split

The west wall of the tower is Norman. Puddingstone was used in its construction along with Roman brick and rubble. Puddingstone is a conglomerate of glacial detritus created by Ice Age activity.

between the lords of Boxted Hall and Rivers Hall, it is not known how the cure - the spiritual charge of care - was originally divided. Rivers Hall gave its share to St. John's Abbey in Colchester. Whether St. John's took turns with Little Horkesley Priory to supply priests is not known.

The priest hut was built next to the chancel wall where the North aisle now starts. The hut was about two metres square and was set about half a metre into the ground. It is believed that there was a door into the chancel which was blocked when the chancel was rebuilt in the 16th Century. It is thought that A.W. Bloomfield, who extended the North aisle to form a vestry, probably re-structured the hut in about 1870. The remains of the hut survived into the 20th Century, when it was used to house the central heating boiler, but was destroyed when the oil-fired boiler was replaced by an electric system.

The Black Death and Communal Grave

BETWEEN SEPTEMBER 1348 AND SEPTEMBER 1349, the Black Death ravaged Boxted. Bubonic Plague, to give it the correct description, is carried by the black rat and is transmitted to humans by the rat flea. It is thought that the black rat came into the country via the ports, and at this time Colchester was a flourishing port, exporting woollen cloth to Europe and importing goods coming from many other parts of the world. The black rat became endemic in the villages around Colchester.

17th Century Gravestone. Wife of John Aldham.

The mild winters of 1345 and 1346 led to an enormous increase in the rat population, which, during the severe winter of 1347, moved into the houses. The straw roofs made ideal homes for rats and their fleas moved onto the human occupants. Plague became widespread.

Black Death: it is thought that almost half the population perished.

As records were not kept, the exact number of people who died of the plague in Boxted cannot be established. However, if the number of wills registered and recorded in Colchester and the surrounding villages is considered, it gives us some idea of what happened. In the years before the Black Death the number of wills registered in the Colchester area was 25. Between September 1348 and September 1349, a total of 111 wills was recorded - more than a fourfold increase.

GRAVEYARDS

The earliest churchyard gravestones were erected in the 17th Century by yeomen, husbandmen and craftsmen in imitation of their superiors who were buried inside the church. These early gravestones are found on the South side near the church porch. The North side was regarded as the 'Devil's side' and was used for the burials of excommunicants, suicides and the unbaptised. This superstition declined in the 18th Century but, to this day, the North sides of churchyards are usually much smaller than those on the South.

In Boxted it is thought that almost half the population perished. With such a large number of people succumbing to the plague, it was not possible to bury them in the normal way and therefore a communal grave was made. This was the age of superstition and many local people thought that the Black Death was a curse upon them for their wickedness. So the grave was dug on the North side of the church as far from the building as possible. The grave was unmarked, but legend suggests that the grave was next to the Essex Way almost opposite the North door, now a window. There were thought to be 32 bodies in the grave.

'He who sups with the Devil needs a long spoon.'

In the 19th Century, when grave space within the churchyard was getting short, a grave was opened near the Essex Way. It is said that many human bones were uncovered. The grave was quickly filled in.

There is a 17th Century gravestone to be found in the South side of the churchyard. It is marked with a crossed ladle and torch. It may be the grave of a rather dubious character, the skull and crossed ladles signifying the old adage 'He who sups with the Devil needs a long spoon.' On the other hand it may be that is the grave of a religious rebel, who was condemned as such.

Patronage and Finance

PATRONAGE:

Although Robert de Horkesley and his wife, Beatrice, were instrumental in establishing Boxted Church and linking it to Little Horkesley Priory, it seems that by 1185, the patronage and finance was divided between Boxted Hall and Rivers Hall. This division between two feudal landowners is understandable, as each lord was responsible for the collection and payment of the tithe on his estate. Thus, they would in turn share the patronage.

The Tithe was a levy on the production, agricultural and otherwise, of land, to maintain the

Rivers Hall Long Barn was the longest barn in Essex, until the hurricane in 1987. (see page 65).

Church. This was usually in kind; one tenth of everything produced went to the Church. Tithe barns were built to store the produce until it could be sold. There is no evidence of early tithe barns in Boxted, so it seems likely that all produce went directly to Little Horkesley Priory, to be stored.

The Vicarage photographed in about 1920.

Rivers Hall had a large barn which, before its destruction in the great storm of 1987, was the longest barn in Essex. This barn was not built near the manor, but on the road to the water mill. It stood beside the 'tenterfield', where in the days when Boxted was involved in woollen cloth production, the cloth was hung to stretch and dry. Could this barn have been built to store the tithe of cloth as well as other produce from the farms?

In the early days, tithe was divided between monasteries, priories, the Roman Church and the parish. Thus the Great Tithe went to Rome or its associates, while the Small Tithe sustained the parish church. Boxted, whose first priest, Roberto, was a Cluniac monk from Little Horkesley Priory, received the Small Tithe only, the share coming from the Prior. The Small Tithe later became the Vicarial Tithe paid to the priest at Boxted by the Rector of the appropriate Rectory Manor. Boxted has always had a Vicar.

The Bishop of London remained patron (from 1237) until the mid-19th century.

In the Church of England, for historical reasons, some priests are vicars and others are rectors. The rector receives the tithes of his parish directly, while the vicar does not, and is paid a salary by his diocese. In the Church of Ireland, all priests are rectors, not vicars.

It is not known how the 'cure' - the spiritual and pastoral charge of the parish - was originally granted, but Hugh of Rivers Hall gave his share to St. John's Abbey in Colchester. A vicarage was endowed before 1237, and in that year, St. John's Abbey gave its patronage - the right to appoint a priest - to the Bishop of London. After 1242, Little Horkesley Priory gave its half to the same Bishop who was recorded as patron for the whole in 1254.

At the dissolution of the monasteries (1536 - 1540) the patronage passed to the Crown, who granted it to the Dean and Chapter of St. George's Chapel, Windsor. Later Thomas Wolsey

ABBEYS, MONASTERIES AND PRIORIES

Abbeys were major monasteries ruled over by an abbot. The Cistercian and Premonstratensian foundations were abbeys, whereas the Cluniac and Carthusian houses were priories dependent on the original monastery of their order. The Benedictines, Augustinians and Gilbertines had both abbeys and priories. In practice, the greatest priories were as large as many of the abbeys.

The word 'monk' derives from the Greek word meaning 'alone'. The first monks were solitary men who withdrew from society to pursue a /...

/... lonely, ascetic, spiritual life in the deserts of Egypt, Palestine and Syria in the 3rd Century. St Basil of Caesarea represented the new type of monk of the mid-4th Century. He was a highly educated man from a professional family who concluded that the organized communal way of life was better than the solitary existence of the hermit. The Rule of St.Benedict (ca.480-550) provided the standard pattern of observance throughoout the mediaeval West. Little is known about the origins of the Rule of this obscure Italian abbot. His monastery was organised along the same lines as a Roman villa, with the abbot firmly in charge. Obedience was the cardinal principle. The monks made vows of obedience, chastity and poverty.

The Cluniac order of the Benedictine monks was founded in Burgundy in 909, and by the end of the 11th Century, Cluny was the head of a huge internatiional organisation. The first Cluniac house in Britain was Lewes Priory endowed by William de Warenne, one of William1's mightiest barons. Other orders - Cistercians, Augustians, Premonstratensians, Carthusians and Gilbertines - nearly all of which originated in France were established in the 12th and later Centuries. The Premonstratensians were an order founded at Premontre near Laon in France in 1120. The order was dissolved by the late 1530s.

held it, and after his death it was granted to Henry Audley and John Maynard. Nevertheless, the Bishop of London remained patron until the mid-19th Century. The Bishop of Rochester was patron in 1852 followed by the Bishop of St. Albans in 1878. The Bishop of Chelmsford became patron in 1926 and remained so until 1981 when the benefice of 'Boxted with Langham' was created. The Duchy of Lancaster, was patron of Langham, so for a time the patronage was shared. In 1999 Boxted ceased to be a parish in its own right, and is now linked with the parish of Langham.

Finance

In 1254 the church, presumably the Rectory, was worth five marks and the vicarage, four marks. The tithes were divided between the Abbot of St. John's (from Rivers Hall) and Little Horkesley Priory (from Boxted Hall). In 1291 Boxted paid £7 6s. 8d spiritualities, some of it to St. Botolph's Priory in Colchester. The temporalities were divided between St. John's Abbey (1s 0d) and the Prioress of Wix (3s 1d). In 1324-25 Boxted church was let and farmed by Little Horkesley Priory for £6 13s. 4d. In 1428 both St. John's Abbey and St. Botolph's Priory were said to have portions in Boxted church.

In 1535 the vicarage (benefice, not the building) was valued at £7 13s 8d. and the vicarial tithes at 15s 4½d. In 1536 those tithes that had belonged to the Prior of St. Botolph's were granted to Thomas Audley. In 1542, Audley exchanged them, together with other assets, with the Crown, in return for Tilty Abbey near Great Dunmow in Essex. The Crown granted them to Henry Scrope, Lord Scrope of Bolton, in 1571.

In 1610 there was only one acre of vicarial glebe, the impropriate rectory being said to have stripped the vicar 'stark naked' without glebe, wood, hay or corn. Nevertheless, by 1650, the vicarage glebe was worth £4 0s. 0d. and the tithes £41 0s. 0d. In 1657 the living was augmented by £10 given by the Trustees for the maintenance of ministers. In 1661, the living was said to be worth £60. In 1720 the vicarage was increased to £200 by the Bishop of London. By about 1723 there were three or four farms that claimed to be tithe-free, but it is not known on what grounds they claimed exemption. They might represent the portion originally held by St. Botolph's Priory and subsequently lost. They may have been a tithe-free part of Kingswood near Runkyn's Corner. In the same year the vicarial tithes were valued at £92.

> Stripped the vicar 'stark naked' without glebe, wood, hay or corn.

In 1810, with the assistance of £200 from Queen Anne's Bounty, Valiants Farm at Pebmarsh was bought. It comprised a house, outbuildings, 27 acres of land, and was subsequently let for £31 per annum. By 1831 the vicarial living was valued at £190 per annum. The vicarial tithes were commuted for £225 and the rectorial tithes for £553. There were four acres of vicarial glebe - including the vicarage site - and 61 acres of rectorial glebe. The rectory land was south of the road that fronts the Vicarage and Parsonage Farm. The vicarial living was valued at £260 per annum in 1863. By 1887 there was one acre of vicarial glebe opposite the Vicarage, two acres in Queen's Head Road let as allotments, and 27 acres at Valiants Farm, Pebmarsh. Valiants Farm was sold in 1920 and the proceeds invested. From 1927 the vicarage received £40 per annum from the vicar of Pebmarsh and a further £60 a year from Queen Anne's Bounty.

Following the 1914 - 1918 war, the living at Boxted declined from £467 to about £300, owing to the agricultural depression between 1926 and 1933.

MEDIAEVAL CURRENCY

For the most of the period, the weight of silver or gold contained in the coin determined what the value of the coin was. Coins were not made of pure silver or pure gold, but were always alloyed to another metal to improve their ability to withstand wear. The amount of silver or gold contained in the alloy is known as the fineness. Although coins may carry the same name throughout many periods of history, they often varied widely in size, weight, and, less often, fineness. Coins could also change value during their lifetime as the value of metal in them became greater than their face value.

As long as currency was based on the value of silver, the basic monetary unit was the penny. Because that was a rather small unit, the Mark (160 pence), and later the Pound (240 pence), were used for accounting purposes, although no Mark coin was issued and there was no Pound coin before 1489. The shilling was also introduced at this time as a coin, then called a Teston.

The west tower of St Peter's Church.

QUEEN ANNE'S BOUNTY

From 1704, the incomes of the poorer clergy of the Church of England were supplemented by a fund which drew upon ecclesiastical revenues confiscated by Henry VIII and payments made by clergymen with larger incomes.

Tithes were no longer paid direct to the Church, but collected by a Tithe Commission in London and administered by the Church Commissioners. The living at Boxted had risen to £434 per annum by 1949. After the abolition of tithes in 1952, stipends were set at a national level. In 1953 the £40 annual charge on Lamarsh and Alphamstone parish was converted to a capital sum under Section 4 of Queen Anne's Bounty (Powers) Measure 1939.

By about 1970, any land, property or assets owned by Boxted church had passed to the Church Commissioners. The parish was still responsible for the repair and upkeep of the church and churchyard, while the responsibility to provide accommodation and pay the vicar's stipend rested with the Church Commissioners. In recent years the Commissioners have been unable to fulfil their commitment to the clergy with regards to stipends and pensions. Churchgoers have had to make up the deficit by increased giving. The various Dioceses have, in fairness to the parishes, implemented a 'quota' system. Each year a sum of money is requested from each parish to be paid to the Diocese for the payment of stipends and pensions.

Incumbents

All the recorded priests of St Peter's are listed in the church.

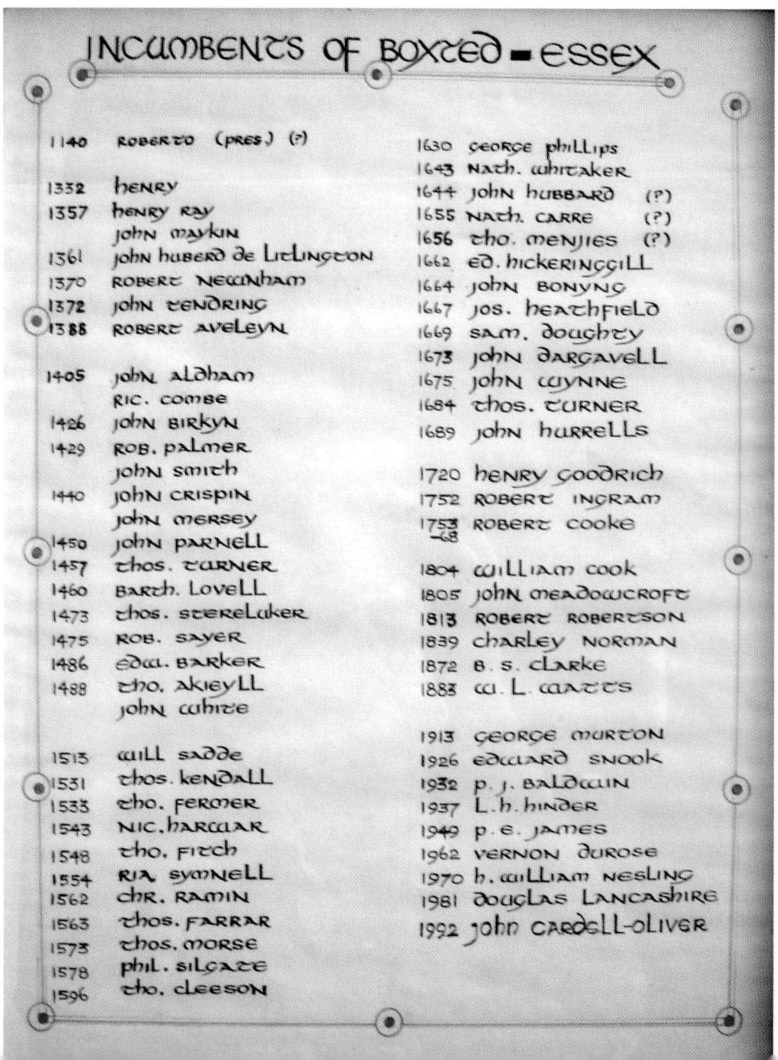

INCUMBENTS OF BOXTED - ESSEX
1140 ROBERTO (PRES.) (?)
1332 HENRY
1357 HENRY RAY
JOHN MAYKIN
1361 JOHN HUBERD DE LITLINGTON
1370 ROBERT NEWNHAM
1372 JOHN TENDRING
1388 ROBERT AVELEYN
1405 JOHN ALDHAM
RIC. COMBE
1426 JOHN BIRKYN
1429 ROB. PALMER
JOHN SMITH
1440 JOHN CRISPIN
JOHN MERSEY
1450 JOHN PARNELL
1457 THOS. TURNER
1460 BARTH. LOVELL
1473 THOS. STERELUKER
1475 ROB. SAYER
1486 EDW. BARKER
1488 THO. AKIEYLL
JOHN WHITE
1515 WILL SADDE
1531 THOS. KENDALL
1533 THO. FERMER
1543 NIC. HARWAR
1548 THO. FITCH
1554 RIA SYMNELL
1562 CHR. RAMIN
1563 THOS. FARRAR
1573 THOS. MORSE
1578 PHIL. SILGATE
1596 THO. CLEESON
1630 GEORGE PHILLIPS
1643 NATH. WHITAKER
1644 JOHN HUBBARD (?)
1655 NATH. CARRE (?)
1656 THO. MENJIES (?)
1662 ED. HICKERINGGILL
1664 JOHN BONYNG
1667 JOS. HEATHFIELD
1669 SAM. DOUGHTY
1673 JOHN DARGAVELL
1675 JOHN WYNNE
1684 THOS. TURNER
1689 JOHN HURRELLS
1720 HENRY GOODRICH
1752 ROBERT INGRAM
1753 -68 ROBERT COOKE
1804 WILLIAM COOK
1805 JOHN MEADOWCROFT
1813 ROBERT ROBERTSON
1839 CHARLEY NORMAN
1872 B. S. CLARKE
1883 W. L. WATTS
1913 GEORGE MURTON
1926 EDWARD SNOOK
1932 P. J. BALDWIN
1937 L. H. HINDER
1949 P. E. JAMES
1962 VERNON DUROSE
1970 H. WILLIAM NESLING
1981 DOUGLAS LANCASHIRE
1992 JOHN CARDELL-OLIVER

FROM 1140 UNTIL 1332 THE MONKS of Little Horkesley Priory administered Boxted Church. In the records of incumbents of the parish, after Roberto in 1140, no further priests were recorded until Henry in 1332. Whether his successor, Henry Ray, who resigned in 1357 was the same man we do not know.

During the Angevin period (1154 - 1204) when Robert Eveleyn and John Aldham were incumbents at St. Peter's, church income both in money and in kind increased considerably.

In 1524-5 there was a parish guild whose stock was in the hands of the churchwarden, Robert Seker. The former guild lands may have been those recorded in 1598, when a Boxted Hall tenant paid 11d. rent for a customary holding comprising a guild and tenement called Eastlayes, but the location is not known.

In 1550, Thomas Finch, nonconformist vicar of Boxted, introduced Thomas Cranmer's Prayer Book. When

Mary came to the throne in 1553 and restored Roman Catholicism, legend has it that Thomas Finch had to flee. The next year Ria Symnell, an 'all things to all men' parson was inducted.

The cowardly vicar

There is a story that James Abbs, a rebel parson from Nayland, had been to Bury St. Edmunds, took money for recanting his Puritan beliefs, and immediately threw the coins back in the Bishop's face. Abbs came to Boxted the following day to preach the sermon, escorted by a large number of Nayland Puritans. Ria Symnell was so scared that he removed his surplice and threw it away, and as it was written 'They would have lyked him worse if he had worn it'. James Abbs was eventually arrested and burnt at the stake in Bury St. Edmunds.

Times were difficult for incumbents during the reigns of the Catholic Mary and the Protestant Elizabeth. The vicar of Boxted was 'deprived' in 1555, and in 1559, was ejected for non-subscription presumably for Protestantism and Catholicism respectively. In 1573 Thomas Morse was inducted vicar at Boxted. He was an ancestor of Samuel Morse, the American who invented the Morse code.

In 1590 Silgate (came) before the church court for being a brawler and slanderer; not wearing a surplice or making the sign of the cross.

The brawling vicar

Phillip Silgate (or Gillgate), vicar from 1578-1596, was reported as a non-preaching minister in 1584 and 1593. In 1589 the Ten Commandments were said to be lacking in the church, and in 1590 the churchwardens presented Silgate before the church court for being a brawler and slanderer; not wearing a surplice nor making the sign of the cross. It seems that he had fallen foul of the Maidstones, avid Puritans, who 'controlled' the church. Thomas Gleeson who followed him fared little better, and was accused of procuring a parson from Langham to preach without a licence.

George Phillips, a nonconformist divine, became vicar in 1615. During the next 30 years the church records were neglected; morale was low, and many villagers including George Phillips, emigrated to America. He left the village in 1630 and it was 10 years before a replacement could be found. Phillips emigrated to Massachusetts and founded a church at Watertown on the Charles River.

Nathaniel Kirkland is recorded as curate from 1621-1623, and in 1643 both he and many parishioners made the Oaths of Allegiance to Parliament. By this time however, Nathaniel Whitaker was vicar and it may be that he organised the petition supporting Parliament, and not

ANGEVIN / PLANTAGENET LINE

The Angevin dynasty descended from Matilda, daughter of Henry I, and Geoffrey 'Plantagenet', count of Anjou, whose son became Henry II. King John lost Anjou in 1204, but the dynastic line continued until the death of Edward III in 1377 and then through the Lancastrian and Yorkist houses until Richard III.

Plantagenet comes from the French 'plants genet', meaning broom brush. Geoffrey of Anjou was reputed to have worn a sprig of broom in his cap. Historically it was only a nickname, first used as a surname by Richard, Duke of York, father of Edward IV.

Plantagenet, Angevin Line:
Henry II Curtmantle (1154-89)
Richard I the Lionheart (1189-99)
John Lackland (1199-1216)
Henry III (1216-72)
Edward I Longshanks (1272-1307)
Edward II (1307-27)
Edward III (1327-77)
Richard II (1377-99).

Plantagenet, Lancastrian Line:
Henry IV Bolingbroke (1399-1413)
Henry V (1413-22)
Henry VI (1422-61, 1470-01).

Plantagenet, Yorkist Line:
Edward IV (1461-70, 1471-83)
Edward V (1483)
Richard III Crookback (1483-85).

Kirkland. The parish registers were very poorly kept in the early 17th Century, possibly because of the Puritanism of the parishioners and their opposition to the Bishop of London.

The Presbyterian Vicar

For a short period, John Hubbard was inducted. He established a parish presbytery in Boxted with the Maidstones as elders, and tried to join the Dedham Classis. With the ending of the Classis movement he retired, becoming vicar in 1644. (See the section on Boxted and the Classis) He signed the testimony in 1648 and The Watchword in 1649. He had probably moved by 1651.

It is said that the vicar was thrown from the top of the church tower by men at arms.

The Womanising Vicar

After 1649 the succession is unclear, but the vicar by 1655 was Nathaniel Carr, who is possibly identified as 'Mr. Lax' who was defrocked and ejected in 1662. Local legend identifies Carr as a womaniser, and when a local woman bore him a son outside marriage, he said he was married to the lady and produced the church register to prove it. When the woman denied all knowledge of the marriage, Carr said her mind had gone! It is also said that Carr was thrown from the top of the church tower by men-at-arms when Edmund Hickeringill was inducted vicar in 1662.

Hickeringill was a controversial pamphleteer whose incumbency was opposed by many parishioners. They were incited against him by John Maidstone Snr., a Puritan member of the 1654 Parliament and an elder of the parish under the Classis. In spite of his short tenure at Boxted, Hickeringill was involved in a number of incidents. At the Quarter Sessions, Elizabeth Nevard said that she saw the vicar strike John Maidstone in the churchyard and Nathaniel Symonds said he saw John Maidstone Jr. in the loft of the belfry urinating on mens heads!

St Peter's chancel photographed in 1910.

In 1664, Edward Warner and Nathaniel Plumstead laid 'violent hands on the vicar' when he refused to conduct a burial service for Ann Dymon because she never went to church. Later that same month there was a near riot at a burial at which Hickeringill was officiating when a child and the Book of Common Prayer were thrown into the open grave. Not surprisingly Hickeringill resigned towards the end of the year but continued to live in the village until his death.

The tombstone of Mary Harriet Lay, wife of Mark Lay. She died in childbirth in 1858 aged 27.

Henry Goodrick, vicar from 1723-47, was resident, and held divine service twice on Sundays, and communion three times a year. Robert Ingram, a noted Protestant divine, was vicar of Boxted from 1752-53. Robert Cooke followed, his incumbency lasting from 1753-68. In 1768, Robert Ingram, now vicar of Wormingford, once more became vicar of Boxted. In 1769 he did not reside at the vicarage as he had been given a larger house nearer the church. In 1770 there was a curate who lived in Dedham, and services were held on alternate Sundays with communion six times a year.

By 1790 the new vicar, William Cook, lived at the vicarage house in Wormingford but a large sum of money was donated by a local benefactor to make the vicarage at Boxted suitable for the incumbent. William Cook came to live in Boxted around 1800.

Hickeringill was officiating when a child and the Book of Common Prayer were thrown into the open grave.

John Meadowcroft became vicar in 1805. He is best remembered by the educational work undertaken by his daughters who established a Dame school at Verandah Cottage, now Packwood, in Church Street. The Dame School was what we might today call an informal day care centre. It involved parents leaving their children with a neighbourhood lady (a 'dame', as such ladies were then called) who would teach the children their letters, numbers and prayers, while she went about her daily household tasks

The tragic vicar

Robert Robertson was vicar of Boxted from 1813 until 1835. Unlike his predecessors, Robertson was an early Anglo-Catholic and was not popular in the parish. There was a long running feud between him and John Joscelyn of Boxted Hall.

Added to his unpopularity in the village, Robert Robertson experienced a tragic family life. He had already lost one son, Thomas, aged 13, in 1810 before he came to Boxted. In 1829 William died aged 23, followed the next year by the death of another son, Rev. Charles, aged 28. Two years later, in 1832, he buried two sons, Septimus and Francis, 12 and 22 respectively, and his daughter, Sarah, aged 22. Both Robert and his wife Mary died in 1835. The last survivor of the seven children, another Thomas, died in 1843 aged 43.

In 1832 the Rev. Charles Norman, one of Boxted's most celebrated vicars, was inducted. During his incumbency many improvements were made to the church including the construction of the West gallery. He was also largely responsible for the building of the school in 1837, and its early success.

Other respected and popular clergy were the Rev. W.L. Watts and the Rev. George Murton.

Congregations

DURING MEDIAEVAL TIMES (1154 - 1485), and particularly in the Angevin period, church attendance was obligatory. Refusal to go to church could attract a fine. Benjamin Clere who lived at Cleves was fined two pence. (Cleves was a large merchant's house on the corner of Gulson's Lane and Church Street.) Some relaxation of this rule applied after the Reformation, but with the establishment of the Church of England by Elizabeth I, the rule was re-introduced.

Church attendance was obligatory. Refusal to go to church could attract a fine.

There would not have been any seating in the church at this time - the congregation having to stand throughout the service. Before the Reformation, many of the services that included the Latin Mass lasted over two hours, which, with the standing, put quite a strain on many of the congregation. Later, substantial landowners who paid the tithe were allowed to bring chairs to sit on.

Records of church attendance were not kept during the 17th and 18th Centuries, but in 1851 the attendance was 164 at the morning service, and 210 in the afternoon. The minister claimed that this was below average, blaming it on an outbreak of influenza at the time. After the 1914-18 war there was a sharp decline in church attendance. Records for one Sunday in 1934 show eight people attending Morning Prayer and 12 at Evensong. Congregation numbers improved during the Second World War with an average of 40 at Morning Prayer and 25 in the evenings. During the 1950s church congregations again declined until today, when the Sunday service is attended by an average of 50 people, although Festival services are better attended.

Before the Reformation, many of the services that included the Latin Mass, lasted over two hours.

Vicarage House

Mothers' Union Tea Party in the Vicarage garden (June 1936).

ALTHOUGH A VICARAGE WAS endowed before 1237, there is no record of a vicarage house. There was a vicarage house in 1610 with one and a half acres of garden and orchard. The building must have fallen into disrepair during the 18th Century, because Boxted clergy had to live outside the village, or in private accommodation. A benefactor provided funds to repair the property towards the end of the 18th Century, and the incumbent lived there until 1980.

A very good description of the then vicarage is given in a terrier of church possessions prepared in 1810 for a visit to Boxted by the Diocesan Bishop of London - 'The vicarage house is small with white rough-cast walls and a tiled roof standing in grounds of about one and a half acres to the East of St. Peter's church and in easy walking distance.' (A terrier in this instance means a book containing the land rolls or list of lands belonging to an individual or corporation, especially the latter. It is an inventory.)

The present house, built of gault brick, was probably constructed around 1820. In 1836 the glebe was mortgaged to rebuild the house. Frederick Chanceller supervised further building work there in 1875. By 1887 the house had 12 rooms. It was at this time that one of the church bells was supposedly sold to pay for repairs to the vicarage house.

Further alterations were made in 1937 and the house remained Boxted's vicarage until 1980.

Boxted and the Classis

WHEN QUEEN ELIZABETH I ESTABLISHED the Church of England in 1559, many of the clergy, especially in regions East of London, were very disappointed that the newly-established church retained so much of the Catholic tradition. Puritanism was still very strong, and in Suffolk and North Essex many ministers wanted a more Presbyterian form of Church government.

Towards the end of the 16th Century the writings of Thomas Cartwright and T.R. Travers were having much influence, and in some localities, attempts were being made to reform the Church from within. This was to be achieved by means of a parish presbytery. This presbytery would be composed of the minister, elders and deacons of the Church. The ministers of 12 parishes formed a Classis, which, in turn, sent delegates to a provincial Synod, and in control of the provinces there would be a National Assembly.

In the minute book of the Dedham Classis it is possible to see the system working and also to see its limitations, in that it had to keep within the law. Moreover it was a purely clerical

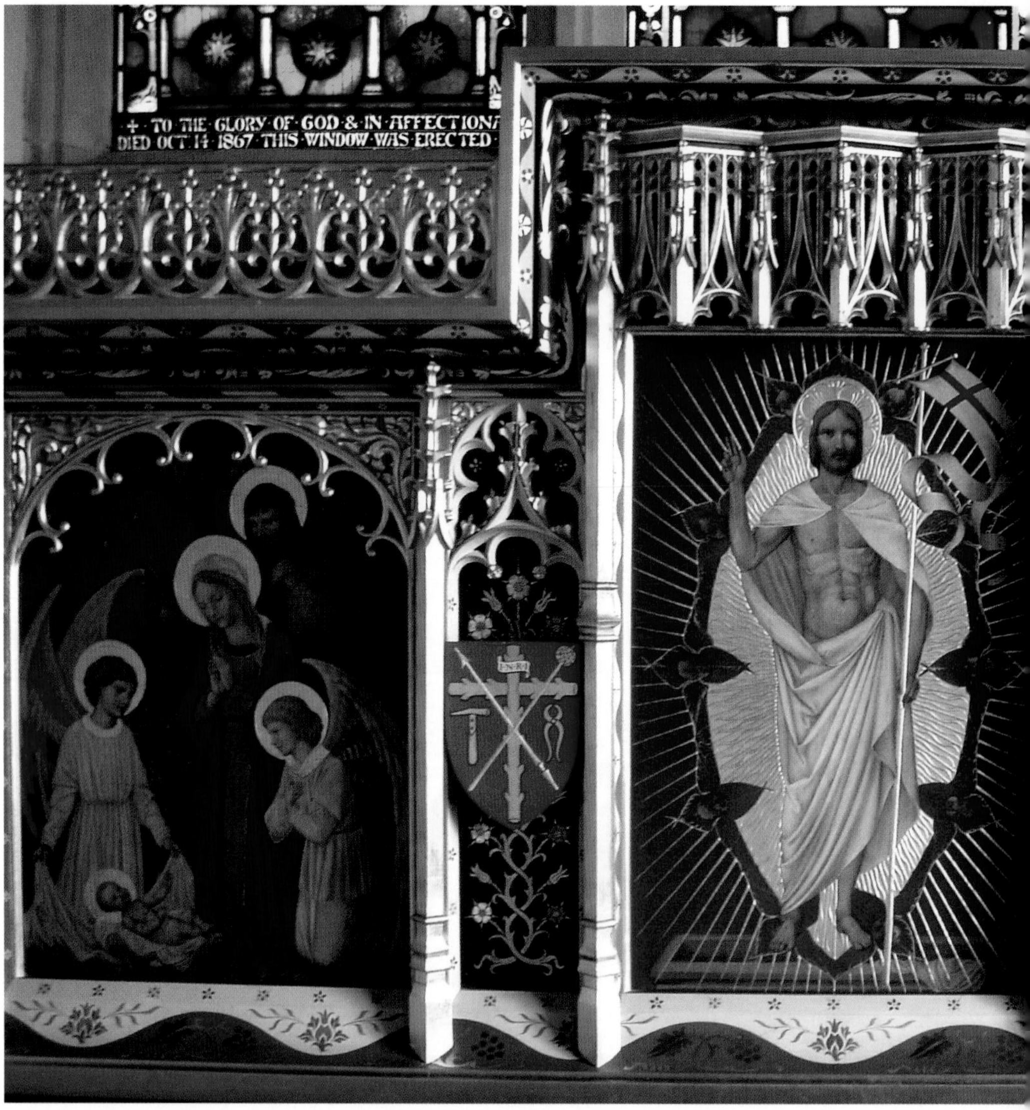

Detail of the reredos in St. Peter's which was donated by Rev. George Murton, designed by the architect W.H.R. Blacking and painted by W. Gales in 1924.

movement with an organisation imposed by a group of leaders. The authority of the Bishop of London was completely disregarded.

Boxted seems to have been in the vanguard of this movement. The Maidstones, who arrived in 1523, were avid Puritans - Robert Maidstone Snr. being a student of Travers. It appears that they manoeuvred a Puritan minister, J. Hubbard, to become incumbent of Boxted. Hubbard, with the support of the Maidstones, established a parish presbytery in Boxted as early as 1580. Soon after this, links were made with a Classis formed in the area of Haverhill, Steeple Bumpstead and Clare (Suffolk). In 1582, a meeting of clergy from surrounding parishes, including Dedham and Langham, was held at Pond House, Boxted, with the object of forming a local Classis. Legend has it that Maidstone's address was so aggressively anti-Catholic, with Hubbard in complete support, that the local clergy left Boxted in dismay. As a result the Classis was formed in Dedham with the minister of Boxted specifically not invited to join.

Late in the 16th Century (1589-90) Queen Elizabeth suppressed the Classis movement, leading to the end of the Dedham Classis, but Puritan belief in the area remained as strong as ever. In Boxted and in many other parishes along the Essex and Suffolk border, the movement just went underground.

When, in 1640-41, a petition for the abolition of the Episcopacy was circulated in the Eastern Counties, Boxted was among the first signatories. In Suffolk the petition attracted 4,400 names and, in North Essex, nearly 1,000 names. The movement to abolish Episcopacy culminated in an Ordinance of 1648 to establish Presbyterianism in England.

By this Ordinance, the Church commissioners were to divide every county into 'classis' which were created to act as 'triers' of the elders of the church congregations under their authority. The elders met every week, and two to four elders and a minister from each congregation met each month as a permanent Classis and to take over 'authority'. Two ministers and four elders in the provincial assembly meeting every six months represented each Classis. Above this authority was the National Assembly comprising representatives from the provincial bodies as well as the Universities.

The complete scheme, initiated by Parliament, began according to Ordinance, and there are lists of the temporary Classical organisations that were thus formed. As early as 1645 Suffolk was divided into 14 Classis but the Ordinance was not published until February 1648. At this time the whole county of Suffolk constituted a province, while Essex was divided and constituted in a similar manner.

In Boxted, John Maidstone of Pond House, and later Boxted Hall, was an elder of the parish under the Classis, and a member of the provincial assembly. In 1654, John Maidstone Snr. was elected a Puritan Member of the Commonwealth Parliament. Boxted was an extreme Puritan community which explains the troubles in the village following the Restoration.

Bibliography

Colchester Record Office — St. Peter's register and records
Essex Record Office (Chelmsford) — Manors, Abbeys, Lands, etc.
Public Records Office (London) — Glebes, Tithes, Congregations
British Library
Colchester Library - the following books:

Victoria County History of Essex
Kelly's Directory (Essex)
White's Directory (Essex)
Smith - Ecclesiastical History of Essex
Feet of Feudal Essex
Reaney - Early Essex Clergy
Oxley - Reformation in Essex
Smith - Essex Parochial Clergy
Dept. of Environment Building List Church Plate (Essex)
Church Chests (Essex)
Church Bells (Essex)
Pevsner - Essex Churches
Rodwell & Rodwell - Historic Churches
Chelmsford Diocesan Yearbook 1978/79 & 80/81
Ecclesiastical tax (Tithes, etc.)
Feudal Aids
L. and P. Henry VIII
Valor - Ecclesiastical History
London Gazette 1852
Davids - Annals of Nonconformity
Emmison - Elizabethan Life
Peel - Second Part of a Register
Matthews - Calumny Revised
Forster - Studies in Church Dedication
Quarter Sessions Roll 400 Easter 1664

CHAPTER THREE

Recusants, Heretics and Nonconformity

Lollards

In the early part of the 15th Century, some Boxted parishioners were Lollards, followers of John Wycliffe (ca 1329-84), who rejected the authority of priests and attacked abuses in the church including the system of confession, penance and indulgence. One of Wycliffe's enemies, Knyghton, a canon of Leicester, complained that in translating the Scriptures into English and thus laying it "open to the laity and to women who could read" Wycliffe was casting the Gospel pearl under the feet of swine. This was Rome's view of providing the common man with the Word of God. Wycliffe's followers were persecuted from 1382 but his influence lasted until the Reformation in the 16th Century. Two Boxted men, including the Holy Water clerk, William Sweeting, were arrested. The clerk was condemned and burnt at the stake at Smithfield.

In translating the scriptures into English Wycliffe 'was casting the Gospel pearl under the feet of swine.'

Lollard

From Middle Dutch; mutterer, from 'lollen' to mumble (prayers). It apparently originated as a pejorative label, taken from the Middle Dutch word 'lollaerd', meaning a babbler of nonsense. Its first recorded use in English is in 1382.

Translated Bibles were being smuggled into the village from the Continent via the port of Colchester, to stimulate the growing demand for lay involvement in the English Church. William Mann of Boxted was forced to recant in 1505 and two other Lollards, Philip Brazier and John Mel, were arrested in 1531 for possession of forbidden bibles.

Aubrey's cottages in Church Street (1920).

From 1528, heretics, probably

Lollards, from Colchester and Steeple Bumpstead attended readings from The New Testament and The Wicket (the writings of John Wycliffe) at the Boxted house of Richard Collins, alias Johnson. This house was Aubrey's, now part of Aubrey Cottages. Richard and his wife, Alice, were said to have moved to Boxted from Salisbury in Wiltshire to avoid persecution. They were arrested in 1534, taken to Fulham and 'harshly' imprisoned by the Bishop of London. Following complaints to Thomas Cromwell they were released on the orders of the King and transferred to St. John's Abbey in Colchester, where they claimed to have received even worse treatment, before escaping to live in hiding. In 1535 yet another Boxted man was imprisoned as a heretic.

They were arrested in 1534, taken to Fulham and 'harshly' imprisoned by the Bishop of London.

Recusants

Four different Boxted women were reported as recusants in 1592, 1605, 1612 and 1617. Recusants were those who refused to attend the services of the Church of England established by Elizabeth I. They were largely Catholics but included some Protestant heretics. There were apparently no Catholics in the village in 1676, but in 1692, two men refused to take the Oath of Supremacy and Allegiance (to Monarch and Church). One of them, Thomas Goodall, identified as a Catholic in 1717, came from a recusant family in Boxted. The family was suitably punished.

Quakers

In 1659 a Quaker, Samuel Warner, was fined for refusing to pay tithes. In 1675 Boxted Quakers attended a weekly meeting at Dedham, and in the following year, 16 nonconformists were recorded. Boxted and Horkesley Quakers agreed to meet at a place in Boxted in 1688. The place, probably the house of John Clarke, was licensed for Quaker meetings in 1705. This was Packwood Farmhouse of which part is now included in Boxted House. Meetings continued in this house until 1747. By 1749 the meetings were poorly attended and another house, Burndiche Cottage on Burnt Dick Hill was used. These Quaker meetings ended in 1751.

Baptists

The English Baptist movement was formed in exile in Amsterdam by a group of Separatists led by John Smith. They rejected infant baptism in the belief that baptism should be administered only to believers and by full immersion. The movement broke into a number of offshoots such as the General, Particular and Scotch Baptists. They were collectively derided as Anabaptists.

Nonconformists

A nonconformist preacher named Rand, who had been ejected from Marks Tey in 1662, took

out a congregational licence to preach at Boxted in 1672. In the same year an application was made for Robert Maidstone's house, probably Pond House, to be licensed for meetings.
In 1770 the only nonconformists in the parish were said to be Anabaptists attending Langham Chapel. Anabaptists were also recorded in 1810. In 1792, five Baptists and their minister, Zachariah Trivett, attended a meeting at the house of Thomas Grove which is now Scarletts in Church Street. There was a summer meeting of Dissenters at a Boxted barn on a Sunday evening in 1829. This was an offshoot of the Langham Baptist Chapel at which a minister claimed to preach to about 400 Baptists.

By 1830 it seemed that some of the Dissenters from Boxted were attending meetings of Plymouth Brethren at Great Horkesley. These Dissenter meetings congregated at many of the farm barns around Boxted including those at Brook Farm, Ellis Farm (destroyed by fire), Boxted Hall and Parsonage Farm, now Parsonage Cottages, and Roundhill House. The Plymouth Brethren also met at Ridgnall's Barn, Great Horkesley.

Boxted Methodist Church

A VISIT TO COLCHESTER BY JOHN WESLEY AND HIS METHODIST followers attracted a lot of attention. John Folkard of Boxted invited Methodist preachers from Colchester to conduct open-air meetings in the village and this led to the formation of the Boxted Society of Methodists. In 1831, Richard Coleman, an ironmonger, acting on behalf of the Society, bought a plot of land on Boxted Heath for £6 from Jonathan Nevard, a thatcher. During that same year a chapel was built at a cost of £350 and opened for worship on January 3rd 1832. Shortly afterwards another piece of land was bought for a burial ground. Members of that early Society included Thomas Beardwell and Thomas Beardwell the younger, William Appleby, William Rushbrooke, John Green, Richard Harris, George Dennis and John James.

Boxted Methodist Chapel in Chapel Road.

The National Ecclesiastical Survey of March 3rd 1851 described the Wesleyan Chapel as having '60 free sittings, 140 others with standing for 40'. The congregation on that Victorian Spring morning was 90 with 25 scholars. In the evening there were 148 although this was slightly fewer than average.

The Boxted Methodist Silver Band continues to play an important role in the village today.

As the oldest building in the Methodist circuit there have been many occasions for celebration. The Boxted Methodist Silver Band has provided music for many of these since Obadiah Willis formed a wind Band in 1861. This became the Boxted Wesley Guild Brass Band in 1898 with Mr. Willis as bandmaster and was the precursor of the present day Silver Band. In the 1930s the Boxted Wesley Guild Brass Band was renamed the Boxted Methodist Silver Band whose primary function is to play at the Methodist services.

The establishment of the Salvation Army Settlement Scheme on the Heath from 1910 onwards contributed many new members with a tradition of music to the congregation.

The increase in population prompted the Church to build a school hall. This was opened in 1910. From 1911 until 1948 Mrs Searles was the schoolmistress and many present villagers received their early education through the foresight of the Methodists.

In 1932 there was a unification of the United, Wesleyan and Primitive Methodists to form the Methodist Church so that the Boxted Wesleyan Chapel now became the Boxted Methodist Church.

CHAPTER FOUR

EDUCATION

The new school, bigger with more facilities, opened at Boxted Cross in 2005.

Boxted School

BEFORE 1837, WHEN THE ORIGINAL BOXTED SCHOOL was built, there was little provision for the education of children in the village. Those from wealthy families had private tutors or attended schools beyond the village. Others who could afford the cost attended Dames schools where several children of varying ages were taught a syllabus limited by the education of the teacher. This usually consisted of simple reading, writing, basic arithmetic and craftwork.

There was a Dame school at Verandah Cottage (now Packwood) run by the daughters of the

Rev. John Meadowcroft, vicar of the parish between 1804 and 1813. In 1818 there were three small private schools teaching a total of 45 children, while in 1839, between 35 and 40 children were in Dames schools and two adult schools were held once a week.

The school in 1906.

The Wesleyan Chapel on the Heath ran a Sunday school for 20 children, and in 1855 a daily school was started at the Chapel to educate the children living in the Heath area. Robert Maylyn built a private schoolhouse near his home on Straight Road, where he taught from 1848 until 1902. In the 1870s the older and more talented children from St. Peter's Church of England school went on to Maylyns to be 'finished'.

The Rev. Charles Norman raised private subscriptions and obtained a grant of £55 from the Lords of the Treasury to enable the church to build a schoolhouse on Camping Close. Boxted School was one of the earliest village schools in the area. It became a member of the National School Society in 1838 and came under the Diocesan Board of Education the following year.

A questionnaire completed by Rev. Norman in 1839 reveals the following information:

Children on the books; 31 boys and 35 girls.
Average attendance; 18 boys and 28 girls.
Annual income; £28
Annual expenditure; £40 to £50
Scholars contribution; one penny per week.

Further information from the questionnaire tells us "The girls have frocks, caps and tippets. The boys have slops. Dames schools cater for 35 to 40 in the village while 80 children are wholly without education."

"The girls have frocks, caps and tippets. The boys have slops."

TIPPET & SLOPS

The Oxford Dictionary defines a tippet as a cape or muffler of fur, etc. coming down some distance in front worn by women and as part of the official costume by judges and clerics.

Slops are defined as a workman's outer clothes; readymade or cheap clothing or clothes and bedding issued to sailors in the Navy.

The school could contain 110 pupils and was financed by voluntary contributions, 'pence' from the children, and received regular Parliamentary grants from 1871. The school's accommodation was assessed as 90 in 1875/76 with an average attendance of 59. These average attendances rose slowly during the last quarter of the 19th Century to a figure of 90 in 1899. The school was enlarged to take 107 pupils in 1895. Nineteen adults attended evening classes in 1869. Some of the pupils attending the church school had to walk more than a mile from home. The head teacher would close the school in very bad weather or when attendance was low during times of a late harvest, or when there was an outbreak of infectious disease. There was always a steady turnover of teachers. The salaries of £30 per annum for the head teacher and £20 for assistants were not very generous and it was sometimes difficult to secure staff.

Miss Maria Webb was head teacher in 1863 followed by George Fleming 1886 and Mrs Mabel Witt in 1899.

Children were not able to attend as gleaning was not yet completed.

In the school records for February 1863 it states that Miss Caroline Mary Scarlett, a provisionally certificated teacher arrived in Boxted - she left in July!

The Education Act of 1870 resulted in a number of changes to schools. The village school, became known as the Boxted Church of England School and attendance became compulsory. This Act and its following measures provided grants to schools that depended upon pupils being successful in oral and written examinations conducted by visiting inspectors.

The inspector's report for March 8th 1871 states, "This school has made good progress but it is not up to the standard of efficiency and requires more teaching staff. The mistress appears to have worked hard but her assisting monitors are too young to afford her any real help. Total pupils - 64. Number examined - 40. 36 passed in reading, 37 in writing and 32 in arithmetic. Total grant payable - £26 6s. 6d."

Although grants were now provided, parents still had to make contributions towards their children's education. Many parents resented both the statutory weekly payments of 1d. and being unable to keep their children at home to help with the housework or work on the local farms. The school record for 1870 states "August 11th - School closed for Harvest holiday; September 11th - An attempt was made to commence school but the children were not able to attend as gleaning was not yet completed; October 4th - School commenced. The Vicar teaching standards three, four and five."

The school at Camping Close was closed when the new building at Boxted Cross was opened in 2005.

Matters had not improved two years later, as shown by entries in the school record. "October

26th - The very irregular attendance of many of the children is proving a serious drawback to progress; "October 31st - A first class boy was sent to find out the cause of absence of children living on Workhouse Hill. Twenty children absent this morning, only five being sick."

The same school record of October 1872 shows that many children were unable to pay their school fees. "October 1st - Much trouble has been lately caused about arrears. October 2nd - Horace Biggs brought 8d toward payment of arrears this morning. Kate Thorpe sent home for the third time for her school money."

Although elementary education was free in most schools from 1891, Boxted parents were still required to pay until the enactment of the 1902 Education Act. Attendances were low in 1900 with many parents being in arrears with their dues.

By the end of the 19th Century the condition of the school building had deteriorated to such an extent that, in 1894, the club room at the Cross Inn had to be used for lessons while repairs were carried out.

"Frederick Minter received four strokes of the cane for continued disobedience."

Discipline was another problem at this time. On May 26th 1882 the school record states "Boys of classes three and four punished for throwing stones in the dinner hours. Alfred Rolfe wounded in the head." And, on February 12th 1883, "Frederick Minter received four strokes of the cane for continued disobedience to the Headmaster, and a warning of expulsion if the bad behaviour continued. Minter was again punished this afternoon for irreverence during prayer together with W. Rogers. A note has been written to Mr. J. Minter, father of Frederick Minter."

By 1906 elementary education was free and children were required to attend school between the ages of five and 14. In 1910 the school was so overcrowded that the county paid for some pupils to attend the Myland School in Colchester. In the same year the Methodists opened their schoolhouse in Chapel Road with a facility for 75 pupils. Children attended the Chapel School between the ages of five and seven, before transferring to the Church School until 14. Schools became the responsibility of Local Education Committees following the 1918 Act. In 1912, the County Council bought a four acre site near Mill Corner on the west side of Straight Road for a new school, but it was never built.

With the influx of fruit pickers from London in the early 1930s, temporary accommodation was provided in the Priory Hall. During the Second World War, Priory Hall was used as a schoolhouse for children evacuated from Carpenter Road School in London. Milk was provided

in schools from 1936, and during the war, school dinners were provided.
The school was reorganised for juniors in 1946, and in the following year for both juniors and infants. Senior students were sent to St. Helena's School in Colchester. In 1954, the school was awarded 'controlled status' and a new classroom was added. Mains water was provided, and when mains drainage became available, inside lavatories replaced the outside earth closets. In 1961 Camping Close was sold to the Education Department and an extra third of an acre was given to the Trustees of the School. School numbers gradually increased and the accommodation was increased by the addition of a pre-fabricated classroom.

Today St. Peter's Church of England School has over 100 pupils.

Methodist School

THE METHODIST SCHOOLHOUSE BUILT NEAR THE CHAPEL in Chapel Road, was opened in 1910. The school was for 75 pupils.

Methodist School with Chapel in the background.

At the time St. Peter's C of E school was overcrowded, and the County Council paid for some of the children to attend Myland school. It was decided that infants five to seven years old would attend the Methodist school, later to transfer to St. Peter's C of E school.

One mistress, a Miss Collett, was appointed to organise and teach at the school. At first about 45 infants attended the school, increasing to about 70 in 1916, and in the inter-war years falling away to about 24 pupils. Miss Collett was helped to teach from time to time by bright pupils who were 14 plus years of age and who had left the church school. She would recompense them from her own income. Also in the difficult times of the 1920s and early 1930s Miss Collett saw that all children attending the school had a hot drink of Horlicks or Ovaltine each day, which she provided. Later Miss Collett married and became Mrs. Searles. She continued teaching at the school until it closed in 1946.

The school is now used as the Boxted Methodist Church Hall.

Maylyn's School

ROBERT MAYLYN RAN AN 'ACADEMY' ON STRAIGHT ROAD, at the junction of Queen's Head Road, from 1848. It had become an 'Adventure' school by 1873. Kelly's Directory describes Robert Maylyn as a grocer, rent collector and day school principal. For a time he was bandmaster of the Wesleyan Band, and after 1894, the Parish Clerk. He still ran the school in 1902.

BIBLIOGRAPHY

PUBLIC RECORD OFFICE — ED 2/159 - ED 21/5028 - HO 129/8/205

Essex Record Office — D/P 30/29/18 - D/P 30/28/18 - C/ME 4, p473
D/P 155/28/1 - C/ME 6, pp. 17-18 - C/ME 40 p53
C/ME 27, p475 - C/ME 28, p355 - C/ME 40, p263
C/ME 48, PP 200, 593, 606 - D/P 155/28/32, 34

British Library,
Colchester Library — Digest Returns Educating the Poor H.C. 224, p248 (1819) ix (1)
White's Directory Essex (1848) p.130
Nat. Soc. File Reports of Education of Council
Return of Public Elementary Schools (1875/6) p68 H.C.(1877) lxvii
Ministry of Education Committee of Council 1871 - 99
Carter, Short History of Boxted pp.34, 35 and 46.

CHAPTER FIVE

THE Manors of Boxted

Boxted Hall Manor

11TH CENTURY - DOMESDAY

Overleaf:
Col. Guy Blewitt and his friend Sir Alfred Munnings R.A. riding over the Queeches at Boxted Hall. Photographed in about 1927.

There had been a Saxon lord at Boxted Hall since 970 AD. In 1008 AD, the estate in the name of Edwin was believed to equal four hides - about 180 acres. The Hall was a typical Saxon Longhouse of timber construction, with a thatched roof surrounded by the labourers' accommodation which extended towards the River Stour. Edwin is thought to have been responsible for the building of the Saxon church. His son Alvric, or Aluric, was lord of the

A view of the River Stour including fields of Boxted Hall farm. Photographed in about 1930.

manor at the time of the Norman invasion.

In 1066 the Alvric demesne amounted to four and a half hides, which later became the manor of Boxted Hall. In 1086, the time of Domesday, the demesne was held by Eustace, Count of Boulogne, as part of his 'honour of Boulogne'. This overlordship is recorded until 1430. The Domesday survey recorded Boxted Hall as having: two plows - woodland for 400 swine - eight acres of meadow - 13 beasts - 35 swine - 140 sheep - and 25 goats.

The five villeins and 18 bordars shared six plows, and although two serfs, a sokeman with half a plow and a mill had been lost since 1066, the manor's value had increased from £6 to £12. During these 20 years, half a plow held by a five acre freeholder had been added to the demesne, the numbers of both villeins and their plows had decreased by one, bordars had increased from two to nine, and its value doubled to £2.

A HIDE

A Hide was a unit of measurement for assessment of tax, theoretically 120 acres, although it may vary between 60 and 240 acres. It is by custom the land that can be cultivated by one eight-ox plough in one year. A virgate was a quarter of a hide.

13th Century - Woodland

The demesne tenant in 1180 was Everard de Boxted who was followed by his son Hugh, who held the manor from 1203 until 1222. Hugh gave Wix Priory six acres of land and one acre of meadow near Cestrewald, Runkyn's Corner, known today as Severalls Lane. Hugh's son John succeeded him, until his death in 1259. During this time Boxted Hall had foresters in charge of its woods (1235), while the crown held rights to oak timber from the woodland as well as in Kingswood and Cestrewald.

John's son, Ralph of Boxted, held the demesne from 1259 until 1303; in 1265 the estate comprised: 120 acres arable - 20 acres of pasture - seven acres of meadow and five acres of woodland. Rents of assize worth six marks and 204 customary works. Little changed by the time of John's death, except that by then 30 acres of wasteland is recorded.

The Mills

There had been a mill on Boxted Hall manor in 1006, but it was not recorded in Domesday. It was probably rebuilt later, since in 1235, John of Boxted granted two mills to Henry of Boxted for 18s. per annum, with timber from the manor woods, and help from the manor's tenants to repair the mill, dam, and ponds. The mill was leased for 6s 8d in 1303, but yielded nothing in 1325 because it lacked a millstone, and it is not recorded thereafter. In later years (1261, 1311 and 1334) another water mill is recorded on Rivers Hall Manor, apparently on the site of the later Boxted Mill, near Valley Farm.

The Manor House

Earl Eustace rebuilt the manor house in 1090, and by 1325 it had a solar at the east end of the hall, with a pantry and buttery underneath an adjacent chamber as well as an old bakery. The site was moated, and there was an upper chamber over the drawbridge in 1325 and in 1610. Part of this moat may survive in the ponds to the east and north-east of the house.

14th Century - Lady Sybil's tryst with the king

Ralph's son Peter, succeeded him. Peter died in 1325, by which time the arable land had increased to 250½ acres, although flooding restricted sowing to 192 acres, and ruined seven acres of meadow. There were also 60 acres of pasture, including waste, 51 acres of woodland and some heath land. The customary tenants owed 10 marks in rents of assize, as well as 54 hens, 17 geese, 20 customary weeding works and 122 autumn works.

Peter's son, another Peter, became Lord of the manor in 1325 and married Lady Sybil who was considered to have been a great beauty and a friend of the aristocracy. Peter and Lady Sybil held the manor jointly. Having been appointed Sheriff of Essex in 1348/49, the year of the Black Death, Peter realised that it was the rats and their fleas that were spreading the disease and ordered that all houses in the village should be torched. This is why so few Norman houses have survived in Boxted.

> Peter ordered that all houses in the village should be torched. This is why so few Norman houses have survived in Boxted.

There is a story that Lady Sybil was a 'friend' of Edward III, and when the King visited Colchester in 1354 it is said that he left the town in great haste to visit Boxted Hall where he had a tryst with Sybil while her husband was away 'on King's business.'

WOODLAND & MEDIAEVAL BUILDING

In the Middle Ages most woodland was managed. Some of the woodland was used for pasture; pigs especially foraged in the wooded areas. Fallen nuts, acorns or beechmast were good pannage (food) for pigs. Large trees were felled for timber for houses and ship building. Underwood, such as hazel, ash, and willow was coppiced to produce poles and material for fencing, wattles and basket weaving etc. Even the bark was used for curing meat and tanning leather.
Underwood also provided wood for fuel, and to heat kilns for industry, such as glassmaking.

The majority of mediaeval building timbers are oak. Large numbers of small oak trees were required, together with hazel, etc. for the infilling of panels. Rackham has estimated that a typical Suffolk farmhouse (which is rather larger than average) was made from some 330 trees. Of these only three trees were as much as 18 inches in diameter, half were less than nine inches and one in 10 was as small as six inches. Outsize timbers, which were often brought considerable distances, were used in large prestigious buildings such as royal castles and cathedrals. Pine was imported from Norway and the Baltic, even in the Middle Ages.

BOXTED HALL SCANDAL

In the winter of 1856 the butler of Boxted Hall eloped with one of the daughters of Pond House.

Earlier, in 1852, Mark Lay of Pond House and his brother-in-law John Brickwood Royce who lived at the Hall led an unsuccessful revolt against the payment of tithes to Boxted Church.

Lay agreed to take responsibility for the consequences of their action on condition that the exonerated Royce bring up Lay's five children by his first wife, Mary, who had died. Lay, along with his second wife Elizabeth and their two children exiled himself to Melbourne, Australia without paying his dues. Mark Lay's name is still officially recorded on the Tithe roll as having £160 outstanding.

Mary's children were brought up at Pond House by a governess and nurses, overseen by their doting Aunt, the childless Marian Royce, who continued to live at the Hall with her husband John.

One of the Lay children, Ellen who was also known by the nickname 'Gommie', fell for a young butler at the Hall; Robert Spooner was the son of the Hall's gardener, James Spooner of Nayland, and had risen to the post of butler aged just 24. Ellen (21) became pregnant and the young couple eloped to get married in London /...

There is a record of the son of Peter de Boxtede, also called Peter, owning an estate at Alphamstone. He mortgaged this property to raise money to finance an expedition with John of Gaunt, third son of Edward III, to the Spanish wars. He probably expected to make his fortune by the early age of 22, but John negotiated a peace with the Spanish king, and Peter returned to continue the family connection with Boxted Hall.

Sybil de Boxtede died in 1384 at which time the demesne comprised: 360 acres arable land - 44 acres of pasture - 24 acres of meadow - 80 acres of wood cut every eight years.

The low arable values, 2d an acre throughout the Middle Ages, probably indicated an extensive mixed farming system with poor arable yields.

15th Century - Hard Times

PETER PASSED THE MANOR to his own son, Thomas, during his lifetime. Thomas died in 1426. The demesne passed to Peter's grandson, Richard de Boxtede, on his death. After 1430 the overlordship of Earl Eustace ceased, and the de Boxtedes were compelled to buy the freehold. Whilst not owning Boxted Hall manor, they were the Lords of the Manor of Boxted Hall.

In the following years the estate fell on hard times, and following the death of Richard de Boxtede in 1437, the Hall was described as 'One Hall of two chambers, two granges and one stable - worth nothing as broken down and ruinous.'

The manor was sold in 1441 to John Rympenden, then, by 1446, to Robert de Naunton who sold it to John, Lord Scrope of Masham who died in 1455.

16th Century - The Non-Conformist Era

Boxted Hall remained part of the Scropes manor of Nayland until 1517, when it passed to the manor of Great Horkesley, owned by Viscount Bayning, Lord Sudbury.

Further investigation of the manorial rolls suggests that the manor did not remain with the Scropes manor of Nayland until 1517.

Boxted Hall 1922.

For a short period in 1540 Lord Thomas Cromwell, Earl of Essex, Henry VIII's monastic destroyer, owned the estate. Later that year he was arrested and executed on Tower Hill.

The estate was sold to an Edward Waldergrave, and following his death in 1584, the manor passed to his son, another Edward. In 1608 the manor was sold to John Maidstone of Pond House. It was subsequently held by John Maidstone Junior who was succeeded by Robert Maidstone before 1672 when the Maidstones left Boxted. It must have been then that the manor was sold to the Baynings of Great Horkesley manor until Anne Bayning sold it to Samuel Rush.

The largest freeholds on the Boxted Hall estate in 1593 and 1598 were the 24 acres at Pond House and 27 acres at Warners, together with numerous customary holdings of between 10 and 40 acres. In total there were about 35 freehold and customary tenants. Some of the smaller holdings consisted of 'ware' land, while the prevalence of three, six and 12 acre parcels suggest a sub-division of the earlier medieval yardlands of 24 or 48 acres. Most of these divisions followed the enclosing of the Boxted Hall estate between 1540 and 1550.

The Maidstone family lived at Pond House in 1523. In 1593, Robert Maidstone leased the

/... on February 19th 1858. They subsequently boarded the clipper 'Suffolk', on her maiden voyage, which took them to Australia. They stayed with Gommie's father and stepmother until the birth of their son.

They prospered and had a further nine children during 62 years of marriage, and left descendants who spread across all six states and two territories of Australia.

Robert died in 1920 followed by Gommie five years later.

Their descendants have never forgotten their roots, and over the years, many have made the pilgrimage to Boxted to visit the Hall, Pond House and the Church.

SIR JOHN SCROPE, 4th Lord Scrope of Masham, had his Barony restored in 1426. He bought back the Scrope lands confiscated following his predecessor's execution. He was Ambassador to The King of Spain then The King of The Romans. He served in The Wars of France after 1429. He became Treasurer in 1432.

He died November 15th, 1455 and was buried in Scrope Chapel in York Minster, Yorkshire.

A DEMESNE

A Demesne was the land on a manor that was reserved for the lord's own use, as distinct from land held by tenants.

Customary work or boon work was labour due to the lord of the manor by his tenants.

Boxted Hall demesne and five years later, John Maidstone held Boxted Hall and Pond House together with 41 acres of customary land.

In 1593 there was a tenant's meadow on Boxted Hall manor divided into doles of half an acre or one acre, the vicar holding a strip called Tithe Acre. William Sickerlinge, constable, of Songers, held 20 acres of customary land on the manor in 1598, while there were 12 tenants of Boxted Hall who had woodland groves on their holdings, probably indicating coppices. A tanner had groves of wood in Boxted in 1571, presumably for bark supplies, and a tanhouse is recorded on a Boxted Hall customary tenement.

16th Century tenants grew rye, perhaps as a subsistence crop - a man left two bequests of rye in 1500; it was grown on another holding in 1570, and a farmer grew rye and oats in 1593.

Harvest in the Hall farm's Church field some time during the 1930s.

The Auction sale of Boxted Hall Farm in 1922. The Auctioneers are standing in front of the barns.

SERFS, VILLEINS & SOKEMEN
A Serf was a semi-free peasant who works his lord's demesne, and pays him certain dues in return for the use of land, the possession (not ownership) of which is heritable. These dues are almost always in the form of labour on the lord's land. Generally this averaged three days a week.

Usually subdivided into classes called: cottars, bordars or smallholders.

A Villein was the wealthiest class of peasant. They usually cultivated 20-40 acres of land, often in isolated strips.

A Sokeman was a freeman of/...

17th Century - Renovation of the hall

During this Century the manor house at Boxted Hall was renovated and the moat was filled in. There is a record that, in 1610, a small boy drowned in the moat. Parts of the mediaeval house may have survived this renovation which re-used mediaeval sooted rafters in its roof. Thus was created a large two storey timber framed house with a hipped roof, a main block of four bays, and two projecting wings of two bays each. In 1661 the house was arranged as a hall, two parlours, a best chamber, five other chambers, service rooms and a kitchen.

A group of farm buildings survives, dating from the 17th and 18th Centuries and includes a 15th Century barn with a crown post roof. The house was separated from the manorial rights before 1903. The barns have recently been sensitively converted into housing by the new owners.

There were 14 acres of land in Shepecote field in the 16th Century and sheep were recorded in 1618 and 1648. In 1661 Boxted Hall farm cultivated:-65 acres of rye - three acres of wheat - 73 acres of grass and hay - two bulls - 11 dairy cows - 58 fattening cattle - pigs, poultry and more than 100 sheep.

Detail of Chapman and Andre Map of Boxted 1777

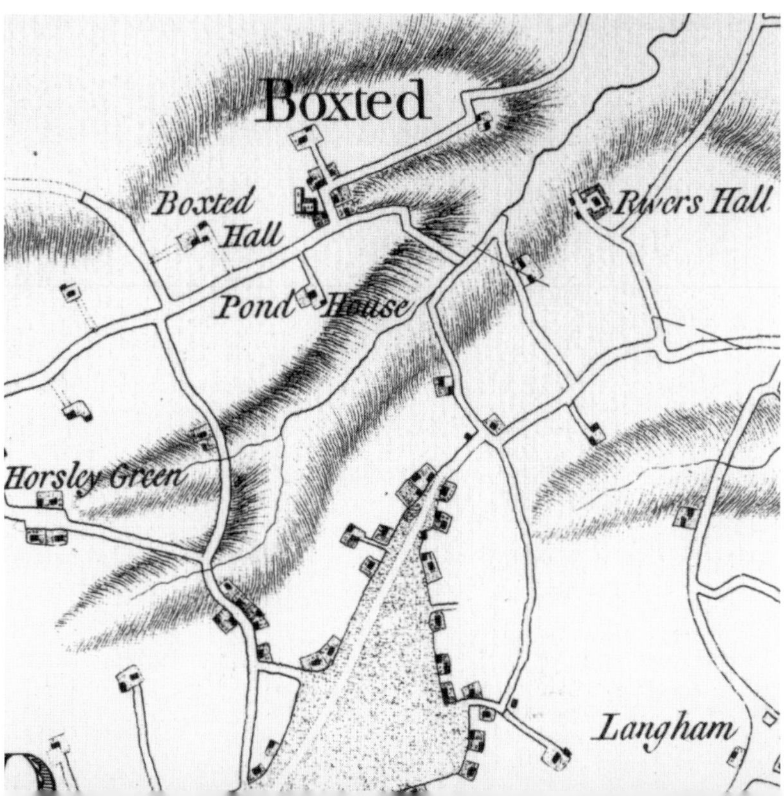

Colonel Guy Blewitt with his prize herd of Dairy Shorthorns in the meadows beneath the Great Wood. Photographed in about 1935.

When the Maidstones left Boxted Hall around 1670, Anne Bayning, wife (or sister) of Viscount Bayning, came to live at the Hall. At the same time it appeared that the land, including Boxted Hall, were sold by the Baynings to Aubrey de Vere, Earl of Oxford. Anne Bayning is shown in marriage registers as the wife of Henry Murray, heir to Aubrey de Vere but later she was known, within the parish, as Countess Anne de Vere, wife of the Earl of Oxford.

18th Century

/... peasant status who was free to leave (and to sell) his land; often owing services or rent, and obliged to attend the lord's court.

In 1713 Anne Bayning sold the Boxted Hall estate to Samuel Rush, a merchant who, as lord of the Manor, bought out both freeholds and copyholds. Pond House was amalgamated with Boxted Hall in 1722, and held seven copyholds by 1734. As a result, the number of freeholders and copyholders had fallen to 11 and 38 respectively by 1749, but the tenanted land still comprised about 570 acres.

Samuel Rush died in 1730 and was succeeded by his son, John, whose son, another Samuel, inherited the estate. None of these owners 'farmed' Boxted Hall - they were all absentee landlords.

Following the death of the second Samuel Rush in 1783, the succession passed to William Beaumaurice Rush, whose estates were divided after his death in 1833, between beneficial trusts for his four daughters, Boxted Hall falling to the share of Clarissa Rush. The trustees for the estate of William Beaumaurice sold the Boxted Hall estate to John Joscelyn in 1838. They then re-purchased the estate from Joscelyn in 1870, a few years before legal action in Chancery released the manor from trust in favour of Clarissa Rush. The figures in the deed underline a considerable profit in Joscelyn's favour.

In 1833 John Joscelyn appeared before magistrates charged with non-payment of tithes and using insulting behaviour towards the vicar. He was ordered to pay the back tithes, write a letter of apology to the vicar and pay a £20 fine. He apparently did as he was ordered.

Forty years later, in 1857, his brother-in-law, Mark Lay, appeared at the July Assize charged with organising a revolt of landowners and farmers in the parishes of Boxted, Myland and Great Horkesley against the payment of tithes which were the possessions of the Church of England. Further charges of publishing libellous and slanderous statements against the Bishop of Rochford and other clergy were presented.

Judgement made against him stated that this indiscipline in regard to the established church had to be taken very seriously. The judge said that 10 years previously he would have been transported to the colonies, but the law now states that only violent felons can be transported. As a result the judge felt that it was his duty to impose the maximum fine upon him. This would be £750 to be paid immediately, with the advice to leave England within two years. This amount of money in 1857 was the equivalent of £36,000 in 2002.

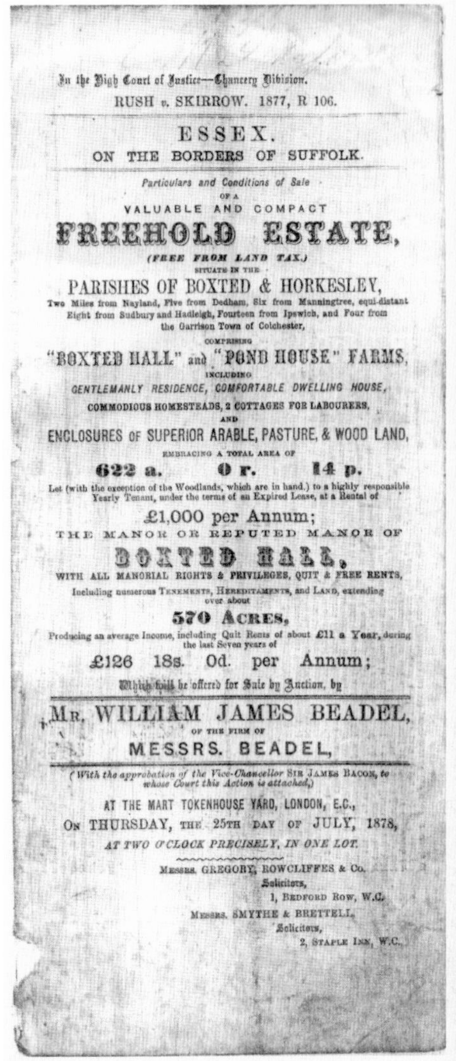

In the High Court of Justice—Chancery Division.

RUSH v. SKIRROW. 1877, R 106.

ESSEX.

ON THE BORDERS OF SUFFOLK.

Particulars and Conditions of Sale

OF A

VALUABLE AND COMPACT

FREEHOLD ESTATE,

(FREE FROM LAND TAX.)

SITUATE IN THE

PARISHES OF BOXTED & HORKESLEY,

Two Miles from Nayland, Five from Dedham, Six from Manningtree, equi-distant Eight from Sudbury and Hadleigh, Fourteen from Ipswich, and Four from the Garrison Town of Colchester,

COMPRISING

"BOXTED HALL" and "POND HOUSE" FARMS,

INCLUDING

GENTLEMANLY RESIDENCE, COMFORTABLE DWELLING HOUSE,

COMMODIOUS HOMESTEADS, 2 COTTAGES FOR LABOURERS,

AND

ENCLOSURES OF SUPERIOR ARABLE, PASTURE, & WOOD LAND,

EMBRACING A TOTAL AREA OF

622 a. 0 r. 14 p.

Let (with the exception of the Woodlands, which are in hand.) to a highly responsible Yearly Tenant, under the terms of an Expired Lease, at a Rental of

£1,000 per Annum;

THE MANOR OR REPUTED MANOR OF

BOXTED HALL,

WITH ALL MANORIAL RIGHTS & PRIVILEGES, QUIT & FREE RENTS,

Including numerous TENEMENTS, HEREDITAMENTS, and LAND, extending over about

570 ACRES,

Producing an average Income, including Quit Rents of about **£11 a Year,** during the last Seven years of

£126 18s. 0d. per Annum;

Which will be offered for Sale by Auction, by

MR. WILLIAM JAMES BEADEL,

OF THE FIRM OF

MESSRS. BEADEL,

(With the approbation of the Vice-Chancellor SIR JAMES BACON, *to whose Court this Action is attached,)*

AT THE MART TOKENHOUSE YARD, LONDON, E.C.,

ON THURSDAY, THE 25TH DAY OF JULY, 1878,

AT TWO O'CLOCK PRECISELY, IN ONE LOT.

MESSRS. GREGORY, ROWCLIFFES & Co.
Solicitors,
1, BEDFORD ROW, W.C.

MESSRS. SMYTHE & BRETTELL,
Solicitors,
2, STAPLE INN, W.C.

Auction poster for Boxted Hall sale; 1878.

Hunt meet at the Hall. Late 1920s.

Staff of Boxted Hall Farm 1925.

Boxted Hall 1925
Fred Giles. Herbert Calver. Tom Gant. King. Willie Ollis.
Riddlestone. Sam Gardiner. Southgate. Frank Ollis. Bob Bray. Harvey Gardiner. Whipps. William
Bray. Graves. Lansdown. G.B. Ollis. Charlie Smith. Elmer.
Ken Lansdown. Henry Elmer. Sidney Smith. Bert. Charlie Carter. Charlie King.

The inheritance custom was Borough English in the mid-18th Century, although, in default of male issue, the daughters inherited as co-parceners. Six women were entered as co-parceners in 1816 and Borough English was still the copyhold inheritance in 1907. There was no widows free bench, although, on one occasion, a widower was admitted by courtesy of England.

Elijah (Ijah) Bray 1929 shepherd at Boxted Hall outside his cottage on Bundick's Hill.

19th Century

The Trustees of the beneficial trust of William Rush acted as lords of the Manor, until a legal action of 1877 released the manor from the Trust and enabled a sale.

In 1815 Boxted Heath was enclosed and some 360 acres brought into cultivation. At the auction of this land W.B. Rush bought some 140 acres and added to the Boxted Hall estate. However, after his death in 1833, this land was all sold away from the estate. Mr. E. Smith bought Boxted Hall following its release from trust in 1877, and when he died in 1914 his executors administered the estate until the early 1920s. The executors remained lords of the Manor until 1933.

20th Century

Colonel Guy and Major Ralph Blewitt bought the estate that included Pond House in the early 1920s. Col. Blewitt was a noted agriculturalist and became well-known in the administrative world of agricultural shows and tournaments. He established a stud of pedigree Suffolk horses at Boxted Hall and won many prizes for his animals. His pedigree herd of Dairy Shorthorn cattle was also very successful.

Boxted Hall farm dinner, Michaelmas, 1925.

In the late 1920s, Colonel Guy and Major Ralph went into partnership with Mr. Denis Carter who had started a fruit enterprise at Hill Farm. Most of Parsonage Farm and part of Pond House farm were planted with fruit trees - the cherry orchards at Pond House were particularly attractive.

Since the end of the 1939-45 war all of the fruit has gone and the land returned to general agriculture. Although Col. and Major Blewitt have both passed on, the property is still owned by their successors.

Some of Hill Farm's orchards. Carters Hill runs across the foreground, the Vicarage and Parsonage cottages are top right with Pond House top left.

Rivers Hall Manor

11th Century

THE MANOR OF NAYLAND (SUFFOLK), held by Robert fitz Wymarc in 1066 and by his son Sweyn of Essex, included that part of Boxted later known as Rivers Hall. It was held in Sweyn's honour of Rayleigh and the overlordship is recorded until ca. 1555.

A SEWER in this instance is a mediaeval servant who supervised the serving of meals.

The descent of the manor and single hide held by Grim in 1066, which had passed to Eudes the Sewer by 1086 (Domesday) when Arturus was its demesne tenant, cannot be traced with certainty. It is probable that at an early date this small estate was incorporated into the lands of Rivers Hall, with which it has often been confused. Consequently we are not sure if the

Domesday survey of Rivers Hall relates to the small fee held by Grim, or the larger demesne of the manor of Nayland.

Knight's Fee:

After the Norman conquest all the land in England belonged to William I, who by a process of enfeoffment granted most of it (except the Royal Demesnes) to Earls and Barons, who in turn granted it to Knights in return for Knight service. England had about 5000-6000 knights' fees.

Knight service was the military service owed to a feudal lord by a knight in return for land. This involved bringing arms, armour and horse for up to forty days active service a year. It was gradually commuted to money payment and was abolished in 1662.

13th Century

By 1210 Robert of Horkesley held a knight's fee in Boxted of the manor of Nayland, and afterwards ownership descended with the manor of Little Horkesley. Nonetheless, the manor had been sub-infeudated by 1224 when William Breton, who held a quarter of a knight's fee in Boxted, granted it to Robert de Horkesley and his wife Juliana, William's sister. After Robert died in 1232 ownership was disputed between Juliana and her son, Walter de Horkesley. Juliana's rights prevailed and after her death the manor reverted to her brother William Breton who died in 1261. His son John, whose overlord was still the Lord of Little Horkesley, succeeded him.

The earliest recorded tenant farms all appear to have been enclosed. In 1219 a six acre holding was divided into six small parcels of land of between half an acre and one and a half acres either in strips or in small enclosures.

14th, 15th and 16th Centuries

Rivers Hall lake (above) and during drought (left).

In 1311 John Breton's demesne of Rivers Hall comprised two parts; that held of William de Horkesley had 80 acres of arable, 42 acres of woodland, two acres of pasture, 13 acres of wood and half an acre of alder-wood, with 52s. ¼p. rents of assize and works, while that of Roger Tany had 49 acres of arable, 10 acres of wood and 30s. 2d rents of assize and works. John's daughter (or possibly grand-daughter) and heir, Maud, married Richard River who still held the manor in 1317. The manor had been named after Richard River by 1391.

Rivers Hall 1920.

In 1317 Roger de Tany's descendant, Laurence de Tany, left his widow half a knight's fee in Boxted held by Richard River. The descent cannot be traced thereafter, but the manor may be linked to the freehold estate known as Packwoods, possibly named after a John Packwood recorded in 1455. That estate, of about 70 acres between Church Street and the River Stour, was held in 1586 by Sir Thomas Lucas (uncle of Sir Charles Lucas of Civil War fame) when it was by far the largest freehold belonging to Rivers Hall. Its attached farmhouse in 1586 was small and no longer survives, but the original house may have been another of the same name - apparently with a hall and two cross wings - that lay on the site now occupied by Boxted House east of the church. The Packwoods estate was the centre of the Boxted woollen cloth trade. The cloth merchants, Bradleys and Cleres, both occupied the property at different times.

SUBSEQUENT OWNERS

Richard's son, Thomas, until before 1346.
Thomas de Batesford until 1352.
Nicholas of Wandlesford and his wife, Maud, until before 1376.
Robert Corbett until 1376.
Robert Swillington until his death in 1391.
Robert's son, Roger Swillington, held the manor in 1410.
Thomas Morsted until his death in 1454.
Thomas's widow married Sir John Wood, Speaker of the House of Commons.
There being no issue from these marriages the manor passed to the three daughters and co-heiresses of his brother Thomas Wood.
Elizabeth Wood, wife of Edmund Dawtrey, held the manor in 1503.
Edmund Dawtrey's descendant, William, held the manor until 1555 when Edward Waldergrave lived at the hall.

THE OFFICE OF CONSTABLE was manorial in origin; he was the link between the lord and his tenants, the keeper of law and order. The constable served for one year and was usually elected on a rotation basis from the farmers and craftsmen, the better off members of the community. The office was unpaid and no expenses given for loss of earnings. The constable raised taxes, kept accounts and presented these for approval at the end of his year of office.

It is not known whether Edward Waldergrave owned the manor or leased it. The Waldergraves' own rectory manor was small in comparison - a moiety comprising just 12 acres of land and

Bill Collins was Keeper at Rivers Hall for many years. Potash Cottage is behind him. (J. Minter).

10 acres of pasture recorded in 1546. It seems likely that Waldergrave leased the manor as relatives of William Dawtrey, Henry and Nicholas, sold the manor to John Ive in 1574.

In 1584 John Ive disputed with some of his tenants regarding their right to remove and sell timber on their copyhold land. A commission of enquiry sought for precedents in the Court of the Rolls and eventually ruled against the tenants who were made to sign a deed of apology.

The Walker Survey

THIS IMPERTINENCE OF these tenants was probably the stimulus for John Ive to invite John Walker, mapmaker and surveyor, into the village to make a survey of the whole of Rivers Hall lands. John Walker began his survey in April 1586, and by November, he had measured and drawn the whole of the Rivers Hall estate. He presented his work to John Ive in the form of a handbook for the management of the estate. Meticulously drawn and

Rivers Hall cottage. (Potash Cottage).

coloured, with the tenants' rights, rents and obligations recorded, he has left a clear image of part of the village in the 16th Century. The 470 acre estate was divided into 55 holdings held by 36 freehold and customary tenants.

Children 'helping' with a straw stack. (J. Minter).

In 1586 the manor had an outer moat. Within the surviving moat is an L-shaped, two-storeyed timber framed house with each wing having a crown post roof. There were three parcels of adjacent land called The Gardens, of about 15 acres 'divided with ancient banks'. These may have been the remnants of an earlier park since Park field lay nearby and two men, named Park, lived in the parish in 1327.

Evacuees Edgar and Alberty who stayed at Rivers Hall (in the background) for a while during WWII. They are standing on the bridge over the moat. (J.Minter).

The landscape was now enclosed with tenements being subdivided into small closes. For example Gray's tenement on Rivers Hall Manor comprised five closes called Gray's Pightles all under two acres. Many of the tenants' farms included a high proportion of pasture, one having 20 acres of land, presumably arable, 30 acres of pasture and six acres of wood. Only half the land of five small farms under 60 acres sold between 1555 and 1599, comprised arable land. Boxted Mill's land in 1595 consisted of 100 acres of arable, 60 acres of pasture and 40 acres of meadow. All the land being copyhold to Rivers Hall, the selling was of the copyholds held by the lessees. In 1593 and 1598 there was a tithe meadow of one acre within the common meadow at Rivers Hall.

PIGHTLE

A Middle English word meaning a small irregularly-shaped enclosed field, or a paddock, or a croft, from which the surname Pickles is derived.

John Ive died in 1602 and left the manor to his son, Mark, who in 1618 sold it to Paul Bayning, later Baron Bayning of Horkesley and Viscount Sudbury. It then descended with the manor of Great Horkesley until Hannah Freeman, widow of Nicholas Freeman, sold it in 1850.

The pond at Rivers Hall.

Within the surviving moat lies an 18th Century timber framed house, with a window dated 1713 and external ornamental plasterwork bearing the dates 1715. In the early 18th Century its rooms were arranged as a hall, a large parlour and another parlour, a large great chamber, diverse other chambers together with the usual service rooms - buttery and kitchen - and other buildings.

In 1767 a lessee of copyhold lands belonging to Rivers Hall was allowed to take three crops before a mandatory fallow, but in 1790 the lessee could only take two grain crops successively before ploughing the fallow - well-hoed peas, beans, turnips and clover excepted. Yields at Rivers Hall in the late 18th Century, when Norfolk turnip husbandry was generally used, were relatively low for wheat and barley compared with neighbouring parishes.

Early tractor at Rivers Hall farm.

The Mills

IN 1586 RIVERS HALL HAD A water mill comprised of a corn mill and two fulling mills which were leased with the mill house and land for £45 a year. In 1838 it was a corn mill, which became disused by 1968.

A crop mark near Boxted Cross may reveal the site of a medieval windmill, but it more likely to be a pre-historic henge. Another windmill, perhaps medieval, may be recorded by Great Windmill Hill on the Rivers Hall demesne, west of Cheshunts, but no physical evidence survives.

By 1503 the combined estate of Rivers Hall had grown to 200 acres arable, 100 acres of pasture, 140 acres of meadow with 14 acres attached to the mill. There was a rabbit warren of about 10 acres enclosed by a pale fence.

Mill House and water mill photographed in about 1920.

Eighty years later, in 1583, the demesne totalled some 535 acres of which 363 were arable and pasture, 55 woodland and 103 meadow. In the 18th Century Rivers Hall farmyard utilised five barns, three granaries, a dairy, a carthouse and 2 stables. There was a dovehouse, and a fishpond.

With the enclosure of Boxted Heath in 1815, Nicholas Freeman of Rivers Hall bought a considerable amount of the land and added it to the estate. Nicholas died in 1837 and his widow, Hannah, sold the estate to William Parson in 1850. He sold the estate to Sir Richard Henry Wood of Rugby in 1882. He was related to Sir Henry Wood, founder of the Promenade Concerts. Sir Richard was succeeded by his son, Simon Richard Wood, who died in 1920. He was followed by J.H. Wood, Lord in 1935. The estate was sold soon after to Sir Frederick Minter whose family still own the estate.

Bibliography for Boxted Hall and Rivers Hall Manors

Sources: Public Record OfficeEssex Record Office
Colchester Record Office
The British Library
Colchester library
Bury St Edmunds library

Books: The Oxford Companion to Local and Family History - David Hey
Victoria County History Essex
Victoria County History Suffolk
Morant's History of Essex
Feet of Feudal Essex
Feudal Aids
Book of Fees
Colchester Cartological records
Calendar Records - Fine Records of Manors
Pevsner
Farrer, Honors and Knight's Fees
Bracton's Notebook
Calendar Records - Inquiry P.M. Henry VII
Rotory Hundred (Little Horkesley manor)
Red Book of Manorial Rolls Essex
Emmison, Essex Wills
Lives and Personalities of the Monarchs - Henry VIII
Newcourt Repertorium
Essex Assize Record (Cal.)
General View of Essex Agriculture - A. Young
Regeneration - H. Rider Haggard
Red Book of Wills Chelmsford
Meagre Harvest - A. Brown
Farries Essex Windmills
Carter's Short History of Boxted
White's Directory Essex
Kelly's Directory Essex
Colchester Archaeological Group Bulletin
Dept. of the Environment Building List

CHAPTER SIX

Some 16th Century Boxted Wills.

The spelling, grammar and punctuation are reproduced from the original documents.

WILLIAM BROCK OF BOXTED GENT. 7TH JULY 1598

To the poor people of Boxted 20s., Holy Trinity in Colchester 20s. and Little Leighs 20s. To Eliz. My wife, my brass, pewter, bedding, 4 milch beasts, half my corn on the ground, half my hay, the household stuff in the house I dwell in at Boxted, the poultry, half the swine and the little bay mare. To her an annuity of £30 in recompense of her dower, £15 a year out of my in Willingale Doe and Spain and £15 to be assured by my son Bartholomew as hereafter; which annuities I appoint on condition that she shall release to him and my son William, Robert Moth and the heirs of Mr Buckingham, deceased, to whom I have conveyed my lands, as by the advice of William Brock of Upton (Cheshire) esq. And Robert Mydleton of Colchester gentleman shall be thought meet. To Bartholomew, my chief mess ... With the gardens and grounds belonging in Colchester on condition that he shall convey to me wife an annuity of £15 out of the lands purchased of Mr John Abell at Mile End. To William Brock my son my lands and tenements in Little Leighs and Great Waltham Willingale, doe, Spain Black Notley and my copyhold lands in Boxted, Great Horkesley and my title in the lands in Little Leighs, Felsted and great W. made to me by a lease to Lord Riche, deceased. To John Reeve my son-in-law and his wife, my daughter, £10. To either of my brothers an agel for remembrance. To Francis Moore my late servant 20s. The residue of my goods to Bartholomew and William, whom I make my executors and I ordain William Brock esq. And Robert Myddleton surveyors and for their pains 20s. apiece.

To either of my brothers an agel for remembrance.

Witnesses: Thomas Thruston, John Thredun, John Youngs. Proved 13th June 1599.

George Gedge of Boxted, clothier 11th May 1592

To my cousin Thurston Ashley of Ipswich (Sfk) my customary tenement called Porrettes with the land, meadows and pastures in the occupation of Richard Barker and John Runck of Boxted holden of the manor of Boxted Hall, conditionally that he pays Agnes my wife for life 45s....... To Anne Beaucham daughter of Prudence Beaucham £20. To george Brundishe the elder of Boxted, my sister's son £20. To George Brewester my god son £20 at 21. If he die before, to be equally divided between his brothers and sisters at 21. To the children of my cousin Gilbert Spicer of London, perfumer, £20 to be equally divided. To the two sons of my niece, Margaret Ward, widow, £20. To Judy Reade £5 and the £20 I owe her for the legacy of her father. Jeffrey Reade at 21 To Elizabeth Brundishe £5. To Thruston eldest son of my cons. Thruston and his heirs my house in Colchester in consideration of much travail and money as my cousin hath taken and disbursed about my effects. To Catherine Meatam my niece a cow. My executrix shall save harmeless Stephen Cole senior and William Bradley my neighbours for a bond wherein they stand bound to Mr Awdley of Berechurch for me. To my wife, whom I appoint my sole executrix, the lease of my houses wherein I dwell with my goods, cattle and corn, bestowing some part among such of my kindred that shall behave themselves towards her. She shall give to the repairing of my town house and enlargement of the same 20s. at such time as the Parish begin to repair it. I appoint my loving neighbours and friends Stephen Cole senior and Samuel Warner of Boxted supervisors and to take bond of my cousin Thruston for payment of £135 to perform my legacies and for their part 10s. each.

To Catherine Meatam my niece a cow.

Witnesses: Philip Gilgate (Silgate) minister, John Humphery, clothier, William Bradley, Benjamin Cleve. Proved 26th May 1592.

Miles Lakin of Ardleigh, gent. 14th November 1598

Appoint "my worshipful good friends John Ive of Rivers Hall and another to be my supervisors, and to each 20s. to make a ring of gold, requesting them to have my name engraved on the inside and to be good friends to my wife that she be not spoiled by her evil children. To Mr Ive my vegals? And to Mr Churche my little lute".

20s. to make a ring of gold, requesting them to have my name engraved on the inside and to be good friends to my wife.

Robert Lucas gent. lying in the house of St John's Colchester 2nd July 1576

...to my elder brother Sir Thomas Lucas Kt. My lands holden by copy of the court roll of the manor of Rivers Hall in Boxted, Stoke(Sfk) and Great Horkesley; which lands in Great Horkesley and Boxted were my late mother's by the will of my grandfather Abel ... etc.

Witness: Robert Brogas, Robert Smith, William Barkant, William Hills,Robert Waylande, John Smith.

The Will of John Ive of Boxted esq. 9th July 1600

To be buried in Boxted church near to the place where my wife lieth. To my son Mark my manors of Rivers Hall with the meadows, pastures, woods and feedings belonging and that live cattle thereon, and my woods bought of Shinglewood, Broga and Fysher in Boxted. My house called the Kings Head in Colchester and my lands in Widford and Writtle shall be sold by my executors towards the payments of my debts, and if not sufficient Mark to pay out of my lands £200. To Mark my wood bought of Rose in Boxted. To my daughter Robinsonne 20 marks yearly towards her maintenance, and my son-in-law Mr R. her husband, not to meddle with it. To every one of her children £10 apiece. To my son William the lands I have already assured him amounting to £80. The one-half of my goods and plate at Rivers Hall in Boxted and my home in Fleet Street shall be sold by my executors towards the payment of my debts, if not sufficient before, and if sufficient it shall remain to them. To four of my men, John Grayt, John Gishingham, Thomas Thwaites, Thomas Bradtreate £5 apiece.

To my daughter Robinsonne 20 marks yearly towards her maintenance, and my son-in-law Mr R. her husband not to meddle with it.

Witnesses: Brian Bradshaw, J.G.John Giol, Thomas Thwaites, Thomas Bradstreate.

P.S. To Mistress Bingsshopp 40s. John Smith, my old servant, 40s. and Eliz. Cole, my servant, 20s.

Witnesses: Brian Br.John Grayt, John Giol, Thos. Thwaite proved 18th May 1602.

CHAPTER SEVEN

BOXTED Houses

Holly Cottage once Heath Cottage. (R. Thompson 2004).

THE MAP OF RIVERS HALL ESTATE IN 1586 depicted 38 domestic buildings, probably small hall houses with inserted chimney stacks. All were timber-framed. Of the eight larger houses, all but one of which were tiled, three had a hall and storeyed cross wings while four were of two storeys only one of which, Pannymers on the site of Perryman's Farm, also had cross wings. Penns, a hall house with cross wings, had two additional ranges - possibly cloth warehouses - forming an open courtyard. Of the smaller houses, 27 were thatched and three tiled; 23 had brick chimneys, and five had wooden smokehoods. There were 30 thatched barns and other outbuildings.

Gate House retains one cross wing of a house which, in 1586, had a hall, inserted chimney, and two cross wings. Scarletts (formerly The Elms) preserves the parlour end of a small early 16th Century hall house - the remainder having been rebuilt in the 17th Century as a lobby entrance house.

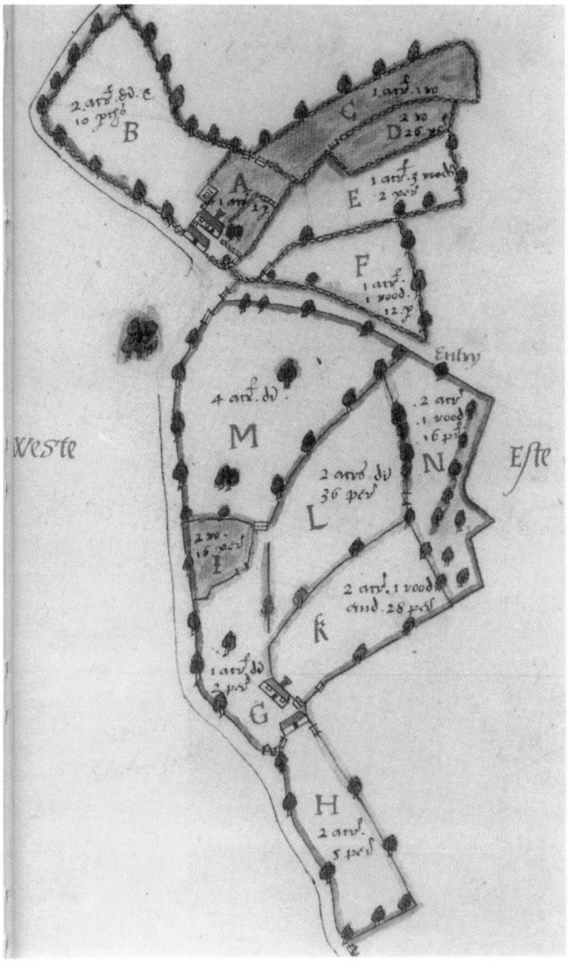

Walkers map of Boxted 1586, for John Ive at Rivers Hall. Vine cottage is marked 'G'.

FISHPONDS

Many large houses had fishponds where freshwater fish like carp, pike, perch and tench would be kept in readiness for the kitchens.

Because fish was a significant part of the mediaeval diet, (it was served on days when meat was forbidden), mediaeval cooks needed to ensure a constant supply.

Carp roe blended with almond milk curds was also used to create a kind of 'mock cheese' that could be eaten on days when meat (and meat derivatives such as cheese, fat and milk) were banned by the church.

Pond House

IT IS THOUGHT THAT A TIMBER-FRAMED HOUSE of a hall and two bays stood on this site as early as 1090. The present house, dating from the 16th Century, is L-shaped, two storeyed with two short wings in the return of the L. The west front has a long jetty which has since been underbuilt. The chimney stack was inserted in the smoke bay of the mediaeval structure.

Eustace, Count of Boulogne built the house for Beatrice of Burgundy and her husband, Robert, who later became Robert de Horkesley. It was in honour of Beatrice's father, Hugo, Count of Burgundy, who died of wounds sustained in fighting beside Earl Eustace in the battle of Hastings.

Robert and Beatrice, his wife, were largely responsible for establishing Boxted church. They also founded the Cluniac Priory at Little Horkesley. The monks, a branch of the Benedictines from Cluny in Burgundy, were seconded from Thetford Monastery. In 1140, one of these monks, Roberto, became the first recorded priest at Boxted. Initially he lodged with Robert and Beatrice at Pond House and later a priest hut was built for him beside the church.

At a visit by Prince John, later King John, fish was supplied for the feast from the ponds at Pond House.

Opposite:
Pond House from the lake.

The name, Pond House, is thought to derive from the fishponds that were made in the grounds for the support of the monks at Little Horkesley Priory. There is a story of a visit by Prince John, later King John, when the fish supplied for the feast were from the ponds at Pond House.

Following the deaths of Robert and Beatrice, the property reverted to the manor of Boxted Hall and was occupied by a steward or seneschal of the manor. The son of Robert and Beatrice, another Robert, held a knight's fee in Rivers Hall. In 1348, the Black Death caused the death of the entire household of Pond House. Peter de Boxtede, Lord of Boxted and Sheriff of Essex, ordered the houses to be put to the torch and destroyed to eliminate the rats that were spreading the disease.

The Puritan Maidstones

IT IS THOUGHT THAT THE LAND AROUND POND HOUSE was used to graze sheep at the time of Boxted's prosperity in the cloth trade towards the end of the 15th Century when part of the present house was built. Further building took place in the early 16th Century, and in 1523, was occupied by the Puritan Maidstone family. In 1540, the Maidstones were the second highest taxpayers in Boxted with assessed goods worth £13 6s. 8d., although their demesne only amounted to 24 acres. The Maidstones completed the construction of the house, the plan of which is almost the same today. In 1593, Robert Maidstone occupied Boxted Hall, and in 1598, John Maidstone held Pond House, together with 41 acres of customary land. Following the departure of Rev. George Phillips in 1630, Maidstone declared a presbytery in Boxted and removed the church

Guy Blewitt's 'Sir Harry of Morston' sired many prized Suffolk punch heavy horses including 'Boxted Confider' whose famous line continues today in the United States of America.

Previous pages:
Horace Mann leading 'Cromwell' a prize bull, with Dedham Vale in the background.

from the authority of the Bishop of London, taking it upon himself to appoint the Boxted priests.

Oliver Cromwell

DURING THE ENGLISH CIVIL WAR the Maidstones supported Parliament against the King, and a troop of Parliament's horse was stationed at Pond House. The Maidstones were also instrumental in organising an 'Oath of Allegiance to Parliament' in the parish which all parishioners were required to sign, or make their mark.

In 1654, John Maidstone senior was a Puritan member of the Commonwealth Parliament, and it is said that Oliver Cromwell often visited Pond House. Cromwell's son-in-law, Col. Ireton, was also said to be a frequent visitor and was very friendly with John Maidstone's daughter, Elizabeth. The Maidstones left Boxted before 1672.

It is said that Oliver Cromwell often visited Pond House.

Pond House photographed in 1932. The bay window at the front was replaced by an extension in 1937.

At the beginning of the 18th Century, Pond House had 14 acres of land attached and was let to Sir Richard Blackmore, physician-in-ordinary to William III and Queen Anne. He was the author of many books, but fell from favour with Queen Anne, being held responsible for her inability to produce an heir. He died at Pond House in 1729, his wife Mary having predeceased him.

Following the Maidstone's departure, Pond House was sold together with Boxted Hall to the Baynings who owned Great Horkesley manor. It seemed that Henry Murray lived at Pond House while his wife, Anne Bayning lived at the hall. When Sir Richard Blackmore came to Pond House in about 1703, Henry Murray was living at the hall. Anne Bayning sold both Boxted Hall and Pond House to Samuel Rush in 1712/13.

By the time Pond House was leased in 1793 the acreage had risen to 149 acres, but by 1905, it had fallen to 105 acres. Notable occupants of Pond House in the 19th Century were John Joscelyn and Mark Lay. Together with John's brother, James, they instigated a tithe revolt in 1833. This led to John Joscelyn being fined £20, with a letter of apology to the vicar, and

Pond House, and extension, today.

being bound over to keep the peace. Mark Lay had to appear at the Assize and was fined £750 and advised to leave the country.

In the 20th Century, the tenants of Boxted Hall farmed the land while the house was let separately. Paul Bridgeman was one of the last tenants of Pond House before the estate was sold in 1923 to Col. Guy Blewitt whose family have lived at Pond House ever since.

Ruby (right) with some of her sons and daughters. She worked at Boxted all her life and had her 25th birthday in 1931 when this photograph was taken.

The Walnut orchard is the last surviving of the Carter & Blewitt orchards that surrounded the house.

Dating the house

The west end is 16th Century Tudor with a small open-fronted timber structure probably of 15th Century origin. The southeast section and the front date from the 17th and 18th Centuries. The bottom section of the north-facing end is 19th Century work while the top section was built in 1925 on the old foundations. In 1953 a flat-roofed extension was added to the west end. The garden wall contains some 16th Century brickwork.

Dating the Barns

The threshing barn is 16th Century while other buildings were added in the 17th, 18th and 19th Centuries. The stable dates from 1753, but a likely 16th Century part probably housed Cromwell's troop of horse.

The Grounds

On the south side of the house lie the remains of a pond, probably one of the medieval ponds. The lake below the house was constructed in 1956 for irrigation purposes. There is an ancient hedge line from the house towards the lake.

Pond House and the barns.

Cheshunts today (K. Barclay 2003).

Cheshunts

THERE WAS PROBABLY A HOUSE ON THIS SITE as early as 1400. In 1317 Laurence de Tany left his widow half a knight's fee in Boxted and it is likely that this relates to a share in the freehold estate known as Packwoods. This 70 acre estate was situated between Church Street and the River Stour. It is believed that Cheshunts was part of this estate while the farmhouse stood on the present site of Boxted House. In 1586 Sir Thomas Lucas held the estate, when it was by far the largest freehold belonging to Rivers Hall.

William Ive, brother of John Ive, lord of Rivers Hall, was tenant of Cheshunts in 1592. He was fined £2 for selling the property without his brother's permission. The property was sold to Anthony and Benjamin Clere who were clothiers. The brothers owned land near Boxted Mill known as Tenter Close and Tenter Meadow where they erected their tenterframes on which the newly fulled cloth was hung to stretch and dry.

Ghostly Murder Victim

In 1607 the Cleres were indicted before the Quarter Sessions for threatening the overseers of cloth and refusing to let them see an illegally constructed tenterframe containing three yards of light azure blue broadcloth. A local legend records that one of the overseers was pushed from the roof of Cheshunts and badly injured. The Cleres, not wishing the incident to be discovered, hid the man in Cheshunts in the hope that he might recover. However, he died the following day of his injuries and the Cleres buried his body under the kitchen floor. The folk tale continues that every year the overseer's ghost leaves his grave and walks the length of the house. The manifestations of this troubled spirit, so the story goes, led the occupants of the house in the early 19th Century to build an extension to escape from the ghost. This extension was built in 1812 by Deaves of Nayland, and is a good example of late Georgian architecture.

Every year the overseer's ghost leaves his grave and walks the length of the house.

Cheshunts front aspect 2002.

William Parsons, owner of Rivers Hall and one of Boxted's principal landowners lived at Cheshunts between 1874 and 1882. Parsons is thought to be responsible for the Victorian addition to the property including the stable block. He was also a magistrate presiding at courts dealing with the selling of copyholds to the tenants after the commuting of the Copyholds Act of 1875. Some rooms at the front of the property were used for this purpose.

In 1882, a wealthy widow, Mrs Emily Collinson, lived at Cheshunts and was still living there in 1899. It is said that she was a great friend of Dr. Jane Walker, the pioneer in the treatment of tuberculosis. It was in the grounds of Cheshunts that Jane Walker first tried out her theory of sanatoria, before moving on to establish her own sanatorium at Wissington in Suffolk.

Election Rigging

In 1914, Cheshunts was occupied by the local M.P., Henry Newton, who lost his seat in the General Election of 1918. Strong rumours circulated following this event. It was said that to obtain votes, Newton spent far more cash than allowed for election purposes. The story told of a great feast in the grounds of Cheshunts for all the village inhabitants and promises from Newton of even greater rewards if they all voted

A great feast was held for all the village with promises of even greater rewards if they all voted for him!

for him! We still have scandals of election expenses today, though not confined to Boxted.

Dating the house

The front of the house is a typical 'Queen Anne' restoration of the 18th Century, which probably incorporates, at the south end, a cottage depicted in 1586. The rear elevation is typical 19th Century late Georgian architecture with gault brickwork, large sash windows and steps to the door. The north wing is a Victorian addition. The decorative slates on the roof date it to about 1875/80, with ornamental features on the roof ridge and north wall. The nine inch brickwork is typical 19th Century. The south wing is a 19th Century addition. It appears that the upper storey collapsed and was repaired using blocks in the 20th Century.

Similar view of Cheshunts in 1914.

The interior rooms in the 17th Century section are very small, particularly those to the left of the entrance that are believed to be remnants of the 15th Century property. The Georgian part of the house is very grand with high ceilings, colourful covings or mouldings and high skirting boards. A circular door stands at the top of the stairs. The magistrates' room is next to the games room. Many different ceiling and floor levels are found throughout the house.

Dating the outbuildings

The Victorian stables are wood-clad, and note should be taken of the tack room. The washhouse was an 18th Century brewhouse where the original sites of the copper and mash tub can be seen. The garage, although repaired, was probably a 16th Century coach house. Adze marks on the roof timbers can be seen. The building would have been thatched at some time with lath and plaster walls.

The Garden

The walls are mainly Victorian brickwork apart from those with capped tiles which could be 18th Century. The two Victorian boiler houses were used to heat the two glasshouses only one of which remains.

Hillhouse Farm from the South.

Hillhouse Farm

THIS IS ONE OF THE BETTER EXAMPLES OF TIMBERED hall houses refurbished for the yeoman farmers of the 16th Century. The central range of the house was originally a long end in-line hall house, possibly dating from the 14th Century, to which cross wings were added. The east cross wing, which has a crownpost roof, was built in the early 16th Century; the west wing sometime after 1586 by which time the house had two chimney stacks.

The farm, on the edge of Boxted Heath, was copyhold to the Rivers Hall manor, and at the time of the Walker survey of 1586, was occupied by Edward Messing and extended to 49 acres. In the 17th Century it was the home of the Mannock family.

CIVIL WAR SKELETON

During the time of the Civil War, Hillhouse Farm became the subject of local legend. The Mannocks, who were staunch Catholics, supported the King. During the siege of Colchester they supposedly assisted the escape of Lord Goring, the Royalist commander. Cavaliers, disguised as Roundheads, smuggled Goring out of Colchester and hid him in the Cross Inn until his escape to France. When General Fairfax discovered the escape he despatched a Parliamentary force to Boxted where a battle was fought around Hillhouse Farm and The Cross. Relics of the battle have been found in the garden of Hillhouse Farm (now known as Hill Farm), and when building work was being carried out in 1925, the skeleton of a man complete with Civil War armour was found. It would appear that he had hidden himself away in a loft above a powder closet and died of his wounds.

Denis Carter, who lived at Hillhouse Farm was a pioneer in crop irrigation, creating a number of lakes in Boxted. His fruit farm was renowned and later, in partnership with Colonel Guy Blewitt, he employed many whom he accommodated in huts (Tin Town) near Mill Corner.

20th Century - Fruit Farming

Every summer between 200 and 300 fruit pickers came from the East End of London.

Denis Carter bought Hill Farm in the early 1920s where he established a fruit farm. Later, in partnership with Colonel Guy Blewitt, he extended the area to cover Parsonage Farm and part of Pond House farm. While waiting for his apple, plum and cherry orchards to come into production, he intercropped with soft fruit. Every summer between 200 and 300 fruit pickers came from the East End of London. Mr. Carter provided accommodation for them by erecting a number of huts on a small field near Mill corner. Being built of timber frames and corrugated iron roofs, the site was known as 'Tin Town'. Several buildings were erected at Hill Farm to service the fruit production. These comprised pack houses, stores, implement sheds and a maintenance shop. Mr Carter was a pioneer in crop irrigation, and to this end, constructed a number of lakes and reservoirs in the village.

Irish workers at Tin Town.

During the Second World War the orchards were intercropped with vegetables which were sent by road to the London markets. By the 1950s the production period had been extended by growing a wide range of crops including peaches, forsythia and Christmas trees. Fruit growing became less profitable in the 1960s, accelerated by Britain's entry into the Common Market, and on Mr. Carter's death, the farm was sold. Denis Carter's expertise and enterprise, particularly in the 1920s and 1930s, prevented Boxted suffering the worst effects of the agricultural depression. The employment of over 40 full time workers plus many casuals at Hill Farm ensured Boxted's prosperity during a very difficult time.

The west side of Hillhouse.

The four cottages of Aubrey's.
(R. Thompson 2006).

Aubrey's

There was a group of substantial houses near the church, at least two of which were associated with the cloth industry. Aubrey's (Allberries) Cottages is the most important survivor of this group. The present four cottages are formed from two late 15th or early 16th Century houses. In 1598, Anthony Clere, a local clothier, occupied the house to the west which was called Alberes. It comprised a hall and storied in-line ends with a large warehouse at the rear. The eastern house was probably called Alben's in the same year. The two houses were separated by a cartway.

In recent years it has been much altered, and in the 1930s and 1940s, it was converted into farmworkers cottages.

16th Century - Ownership disputes

Part of the timber in the house dates back to the 14th Century when it was probably a merchant's house. In the middle of the 16th Century it was the home of the Bradleys, wealthy clothiers, who are reputed to have owned a weaving establishment near Gulson's. This land was part of the Packwoods estate and the Bradleys were in dispute with the Atkinsons who lived in a smallish farmhouse on the site where Boxted House stands today. The dispute centred on the ownership of the Packwoods estate. The Bradleys claimed that the freehold was theirs, proving their claim from mediaeval records while the Atkinsons claimed ownership by virtue of occupation. John Ive, Lord of Rivers Hall, added to the confusion by claiming that the freehold belonged to him as part of the knight's fee sold to Richard River by Laurence de Tany in 1346. All the claimants had to appear before the Court of the Rolls, and after much deliberation, the court found in favour of John Ive. This ruling upset the Bradleys, and under cover of darkness, they destroyed the tenterframes and cloth belonging to the Atkinsons who were themselves clothiers. Both parties had to appear at the Quarter Sessions where the Bradleys were heavily fined and the Atkinsons ordered to leave the Packwoods farmhouse. Sir Thomas Lucas moved in to the Packwoods farmhouse and became the largest freeholder on the Rivers Hall demesne.

Prayer meetings were held here together with readings from the 'Wicket'.

In 1505 Aubrey's was thought to have been the home of Thomas Mann who was forced to recant his Protestant beliefs. A few years later it became the home of Richard and Alice Johnson, noted Lollards, and prayer meetings were held here together with readings from the 'Wicket', a banned publication by John Wycliffe. Lollards came from as far away as Steeple Bumpstead to attend the meetings. William Sweeting, holy water clerk at the church, also attended the meetings until his attainder, when he was burned at the stake at Smithfield. These meetings led to the arrest of the Johnsons and their imprisonment in the Bishop of London's prison at Fulham.

19th Century - Smuggling and Transportation

A local legend concerning Allberries records that the notorious smuggler, Jonathan Summers once lodged there with Mrs Betsy Siddon, a lady of some dubious virtue. Summers was apprehended, so the story goes, because he mishandled some casks of brandy and they ended up in Betsy's front room. The two of them were making merry one Saturday evening when the constable was called to investigate. Summers was transported to the colonies as a result.

Aubrey's, sometimes known as Allberries or Hallberries from the churchyard.

Gulson's house, Summer 2006.

Gulson's

While there is no record of any buildings on this site in the Domesday survey, it is thought that a farmstead was built on this site in the mid 13th Century. It is not known whether this property and land was copyhold to Boxted Hall. The land was freehold by the 15th Century when it could have been part of the Packwoods estate named after John Packwood who died in 1435.

An early map shows a house of two bays, timber-framed and thatched, on this site with more buildings which may have been weaving sheds or accommodation for cloth workers built between Gulson's and the mill.

In White's Directory of 1848 the occupants of Gulson's were recorded as 'Gentry'.

In the 15th and 16th Centuries this area was the hub of Boxted's involvement in the woollen cloth trade. At the time of the Walker survey of Rivers Hall lands in 1586 these buildings were not recorded. Gulson's house was evidently not part of the Rivers Hall demesne. In the 15th Century Gulson's house could have been the home of a cloth merchant. The de Cleres, Flemish immigrants and wealthy merchants, built a large house called Cleves in Church Street near the entrance to Gulson's Lane. This house no longer exists but the de Cleres could have been responsible for building or re-building Gulson's.

The house is an amalgam of different building periods. It is thought that the entrance porch and nearby timber frame could be 15th Century while other parts can be dated to the 16th, 17th and 19th Centuries with a modern addition built in the 1950s. The roof elevation and weatherboarded end on part of the old building suggests that the house could have been thatched at one time.

In the 17th Century, at the time of The Great Migration, Gulson's was known as Warners and was one of the freehold farms registered to Boxted Hall. It is recorded as farmhouse, buildings and 27 acres of land. Following the ownership of Boxted Hall by absentee landlords, little is recorded of Gulson's Farm. In White's Directory of 1848 the occupants of Gulson's were recorded as 'Gentry' and it seems that the land had already been added to Boxted Hall. In Kelly's Directory of 1875 the occupants are once again described as gentry.

Gulson's Barn.

Mr. Arthur Clementson lived at Gulson's towards the end of the 19th Century. He later built himself a large house, Clives, in Church Street with views over the Stour valley. Mr. Cleminson's father was a student of Fox Talbot of Lacock Abbey one of the world's pioneers in photography. Mr. Clementson himself was also a keen photographer and many of his old photographs of Boxted still exist, including some of Gulson's. One of these photographs of Gulson's, showing the interior of the dining room, depicts an early electric fire. There was no electric power in the village at this time so it must have been powered by a generator.

Later, the Henderson family owned Gulson's. Mr Henderson was a London solicitor whose daughter, Denys, married Major Ralph Blewitt of Boxted Hall. The Hendersons owned the Windmill Theatre, in London. During the Second World War, Gulson's house was used as a hostel for members of the Women's Land Army.

'The Supper' by Mark Gertler 1929, is a portrait of Natalie Denny (inset) who married Robert Bevan and lived at Boxted House for many years.

Boxted House

Following the derequisitioning of Boxted House by the army at the end of the war, Robert Bevan (Bobby) who had first bought the house in 1938, then married Natalie Sieveking (neé Denny) in 1947. Together they began the five decades where Boxted House not only royally entertained many artists and writers, but became the home of a fine modern art collection. An important part of the collection were paintings by the Camden Town Group formed just prior to the First World War by Spencer Gore, Walter Sickert, Harold Gilman, Charles Ginner and Robert Bevan who was Bobby Bevan's father.

East Anglian painters were prominent in the collection, notably Sir Cedric Morris and Lett Haines who ran the Art School, Benton End on the outskirts of Hadleigh. There was also an excellent group of paintings by John Nash.

Natalie Bevan, herself an artist, exhibited paintings and ceramics in Colchester and London. She brought to the Bevan Collection the now very well known portrait of herself in 1929 titled 'The Supper' /...

/... by Mark Gertler.

This painting, along with much of the collection, has frequently been shown at major galleries including the Tate, and of course at the Minories, Colchester as well as the Gainsborough Galleries.

Neo-classic Boxted House, c1828, has been sensitively added to in 2002 by the new owners, Jacky and Robin Budenberg.

Art in Boxted House clockwise from right:
'Ponds in winter' by John Nash, 1959.
The dining room at Boxted House, 1975 including a Robert Bevan landscape.
'Ploughing' by Robert Bevan above the drawing room fireplace, 1975.
'Threshing machine' by John Nash, 1914.

A portrait of William Fisher Hobbs (Page 44) hangs in the Farmers Club, Whitehall, London.

Boxted Lodge

The house was probably built in 1792 by William Fisher Hobbs as a two storeyed brick house. (See page 44) The east end was rebuilt in the 19th Century as a four bay block with a Tuscan portico. Further remodelling followed in the mid 19th Century. Col. A.H. Lefroy added a third storey to the east end and raised the original roof in 1888.

Opposite: Barritts Farm, from the front in 1907 and the back today.

William Fisher Hobbs was the first Essex man to breed Suffolk Punch horses. He also kept Leicester sheep, Hereford cattle, prize-winning Essex pigs and hosted the Royal Agricultural Society's trials of reaping machines and steam cultivators in 1856.

The family of Col. A.H. Lefroy, who bought Boxted Lodge in 1833, became central figures in the social and institutional life of the village. The Silver Jubilee fete of 1935 and the Coronation celebrations in 1937 were held in the park of Boxted Lodge. The village football team played at Boxted Lodge in the 1920s and '30s. They still retain the name of the Boxted Lodgers to this day.

Barritts Farm

ALFRED WILLIAM SEXTON *came to Boxted from London in 1915 on his own to grow vegetables for the London markets. He hired a field near Ellis Farm. He married Violet Kate Lucking, whose brother lived at Priory House, Straight Road .*

In 1917 Alfred William, his father, mother and brothers purchased Plains Farm, (his brothers leaving in 1922 for Frating Hall).

In 1919 Alfred William purchased Barritts Farm, Ellis Farm and Boxted Lodge lands, and started on his own building up a 450 acre market garden.

Between 1920 and the second war he employed upwards of 20 men, and 20 to 30 women on a regular basis.

He acquired or built 16 cottages to house all the men during the depression years.

Alfred William Sexton's sons hired up to six railway wagons five nights a week to take produce to London from North Station, Colchester. He also employed two lorries solely to collect horse manure from Colchester Barracks, until the outbreak of the second World War. Three horse men looked after 14 cart horses.

Alfred William Sexton and his wife had five sons and one daughter (who died aged eight).

The family now farm over 6,000 acres in East Anglia.

Early picture of Clives.

The trees have grown up around Clives today.

GEORGE BOWLES

A notable and interesting man who lived at Clives for ten years just after the Second World War was Commander George Bowles. This remarkable person joined the Navy and sailed 'before the mast' as a midshipman in the 1890's before leaving the Navy to go up to Cambridge. There he took an honours degree in history, became President of the Union, Editor of Granta and President of the A.D.C. Later he was called to the Bar, and became an M.P. He returned to the Navy during both World Wars.

His sister, Sydney married Lord Redesdale and he was therefore Uncle to Nancy Mitford and her siblings, of whom only the Duchess of Devonshire survives. He died in Malta in 1955, and is buried in Boxted Churchyard.

CHAPTER EIGHT

BOXTED Cottages

Boxted's landmarks

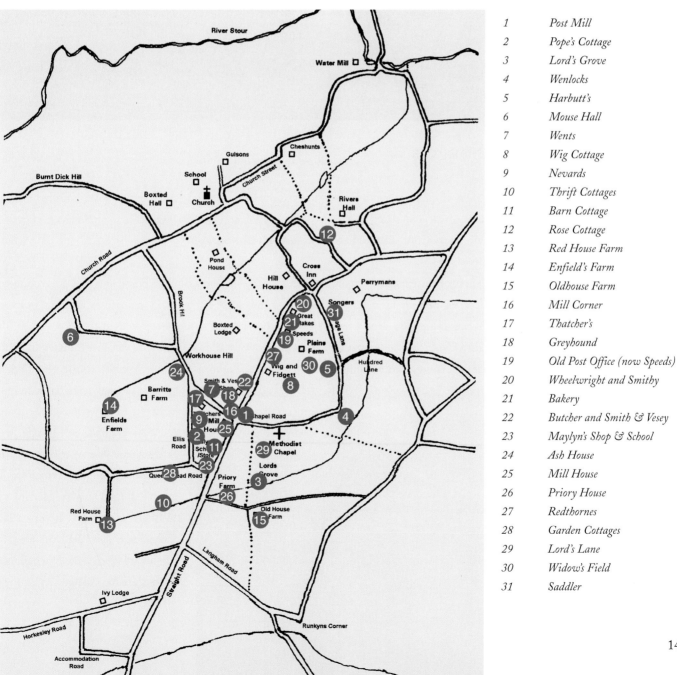

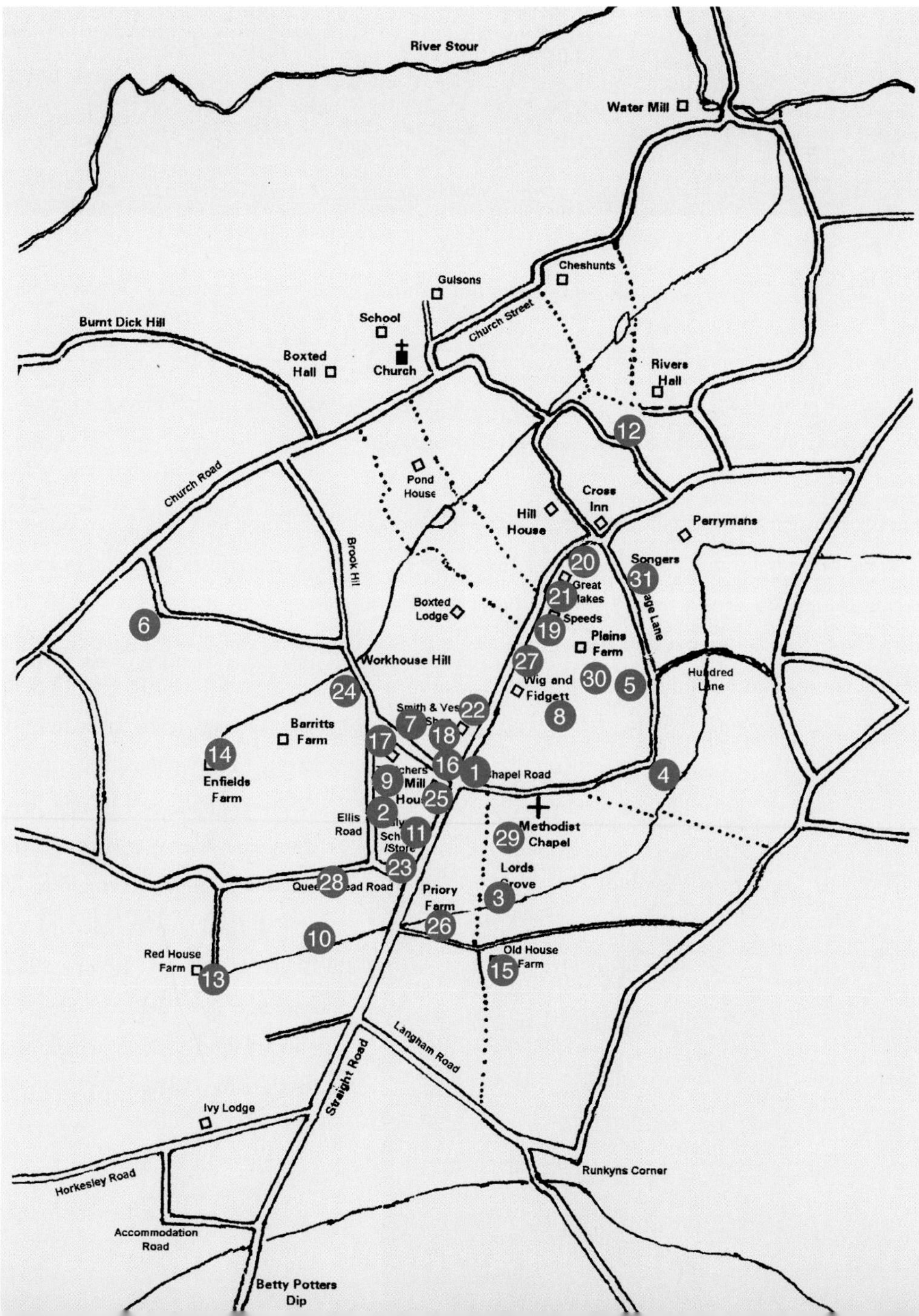

1	*Post Mill*
2	*Pope's Cottage*
3	*Lord's Grove*
4	*Wenlocks*
5	*Harbutt's*
6	*Mouse Hall*
7	*Wents*
8	*Wig Cottage*
9	*Nevards*
10	*Thrift Cottages*
11	*Barn Cottage*
12	*Rose Cottage*
13	*Red House Farm*
14	*Enfield's Farm*
15	*Oldhouse Farm*
16	*Mill Corner*
17	*Thatcher's*
18	*Greyhound*
19	*Old Post Office (now Speeds)*
20	*Wheelwright and Smithy*
21	*Bakery*
22	*Butcher and Smith & Vesey*
23	*Maylyn's Shop & School*
24	*Ash House*
25	*Mill House*
26	*Priory House*
27	*Redthornes*
28	*Garden Cottages*
29	*Lord's Lane*
30	*Widow's Field*
31	*Saddler*

Songers Cottage: *the oldest timber-framed domestic building in Essex dating from 1280. (R. Thompson 2006).*

Songers

Most of the cottages in Boxted built in the late 17th and 18th Centuries, were timber framed, with brick and slated cottages in the 19th Century. The exceptions are Songers, Harbutts, Wenlocks Cottage and Hollie (formerly Heath) cottages.

Many of the early cottages were burnt to stop the spread of the Black Death in 1349. Songers Cottage in Cage Lane is a survivor and is the oldest timber-framed domestic building in Essex, dating from 1280. It is a small two-bayed aisled hall with a two-storeyed chamber end. In the 14th Century an aisled bay and storeyed end were added. The house was divided laterally in the 16th Century and a chimney stack inserted. The open lap notch joints in the roof timbers indicate a date of about 1250 for the original frame. In the 14th Century the seneschal or steward of Rivers Hall occupied the cottage. In 1586 William Sickerlinge lived at Songers. He was one of the ringleaders of the entitlement revolt against John Ive which led to the Walker survey of Rivers Hall. Sickerlinge also held 36 acres of customary land, some of which now forms the King George Playing Field.

Brook Farm 1930.

William died in 1599 when his age was given as '100 years or thereabouts'. After his death, his son, John Sickerlinge the first village 'constable' lived in the cottage.

Vine Cottage and Brook Farm

These are all small later 15th Century hall houses with service and chamber ends and crown post roofs although the service end at Brook Farm has been demolished. Vine Cottage is the most elaborate with a moulded crown post and serpentine braces. All three houses had floors and chimney stacks inserted in the 16th Century. The chimneys at Brook Farm and Vine Cottage replaced wooden smoke hoods.

Vine Cottage 1984.

Harbutts and Wenlocks Cottages

The other two cottages in Cage Lane, Harbutts and Wenlocks, are early Tudor but it is likely that cottages were built on these sites 100 years earlier. Both cottages contain mediaeval timbers although the overall design is Tudor. Wenlocks was a simple hall house with only a single storeyed service end. By 1598, when it was a small copyhold farm called Sewards, a stack had been inserted and the western end of the hall floored.

Wenlocks Cottage.

It was the route Boudicca took when she sacked Colchester in AD 61.

The reason that these very old cottages are found in Cage Lane is that the main route to Colchester was nearby. Before the enclosure of Boxted Heath and the establishment of 'Straight Road', the unmade road to Colchester started near The Cross, proceeded just west of Cage Lane, passed near the present site of the Methodist Chapel, across the fields before it joined the present Langham Road. It continued across land, once the Cestrewald now White House Farm, arriving at the bottom of East Hill in Colchester. Legend has it that this was the route Boudicca took when she sacked Colchester in AD 61. Two newly built cottages along the lane past the Methodist Church are probably built on sites of old 15th Century cottages.

Lord's Grove

Another cottage in this area that probably dates back to Tudor times is Lord's Grove. This is another timber-framed building with a thatched roof as a later addition. Robert Gilder, one of the contributors to the Boxted Charities, once owned this cottage. On his death he left Lord's Grove, two other cottages, a small parcel of land and a small wood to the parish with instructions that the income from the properties was to be used for the benefit of the poor widows of the parish. The cottages and wood were sold at the beginning of the 19th Century, and the land, known later as Widow's Field, was sold in 1956, the proceeds being invested for the original purpose of the charity.

Straight Road at the junction of Langham Road.

Two further cottages are probably Tudor in origin, Hollie Cottage and Box Cottage. Both properties are timber-framed under a thatched roof, but in recent years both have been extensively modernised. Hollie Cottage was once called Heath Cottage and there is a story that when 'Straight Road' was made, a ploughman with a pair of horses drew the line of the road by ploughing a furrow from Heath Cottage to Betty Potter's Dip and back again.

17th Century Cottages

An early photograph of Straight Road.

Many of the remaining cottages in Boxted were built on the edge of the heath from the area of the Cross in almost a straight line to Great Horkesley Plantation. This is why some of the cottages are situated in between roads, with quite long approach drives. Some of these cottages were weavers' cottages, but most were the homes of farm workers. Although originally all the cottages were copyhold to the manors, later they were 'tied' to the farms. The majority are timber-framed under thatched roofs, but have been extensively modernised in recent years. There is a story regarding the 17th Century cottages when the Baynings owned Rivers Hall; they were given the wrecks of some Dutch ships that had been washed up on the east coast. The timber was used to build these cottages. It is true that many of the beams in the cottages have been used before; one can see the tenons have been made for other timbers to pass through. The best of these cottages are Wents, Wig Cottage, Nevards, Thrift Cottages, Barn Cottages, Popes and Rose Cottage in Red House Lane although this last cottage may date back to the 16th Century. A variation on these thatched cottages is a thatched bungalow at Ellis Farm. This is sometimes referred to as Ellis farmhouse. The original farmhouse probably met its end in the 18th Century. Bungalows were introduced to this country in the 19th Century, an import from India. It is therefore likely that this particular bungalow was

Timber from the wrecks of Dutch ships washed up on the East coast was used to build these cottages.

Nevards 2006.

Bundook cottage looks over the Stour Valley and was once two farm cottages for Boxted Hall Farm.

Below: The Wheelwrights House.

Centre: Mill House.

Bottom: Box Cottage, Straight Road.

Left: Oak Cottage, Chapel Road.

Below: Rose Cottage.

Bottom: Medlars Cottage.

built around 1820. Before its destruction by fire in 1983, Ellis Farm had a first-class timber-framed thatched threshing barn, probably of Tudor origin and it is likely that the original farmhouse was also Tudor.

In the 18th Century when the population of Boxted was about 500, it is known that a number of thatched cottages were built to house farm workers. This type of development contributed to the sprawling nature of the village. The population of the village rose from 558 in 1800 to 935 in 1863. Terraces of thatched cottages, consisting of up to six lets were built on farms. Accommodation was 'one up; one down' with a communal kitchen and bread oven at the rear. An illustration of such a cottage, much modernised can be found just past the Methodist Church.

Popes Cottage.

During the 19th Century several brick and slated homes were built. Most of these were semi-detached, or in the case of Garden Cottages in Queen's Head Road, terraced. The majority of these Victorian cottages have now been converted into detached homes. An exception to this is probably 'Speeds' on Straight Road, which still remains semi-detached.

Mouse Hall

THERE ARE A NUMBER OF LOCAL STORIES about some of these cottages, but two of the cottages no longer exist. Both properties were situated in what is now Green Lane, once Wet Lane. About three quarters of the way down Green Lane almost into Great Horkesley was a thatched bungalow known as Mouse Hall. In about 1880 it was occupied by an eccentric gentleman by the name of Isaiah Abraham. He had a great love of wildlife, particularly the mouse. It is said that on passing Mouse Hall one could hear the squealing and rustling of mice. The thatch of the cottage was alive with them, and when the door opened armies of them marched out. In reality it was probably not so bad, but local rumour exaggerated the story. The cottage was cleaned up and modernised just after the war, and then in the 1970's it was destroyed by fire.

The thatch of the cottage was alive with mice, and when the door was opened armies of them marched out.

The other cottage was almost opposite the entrance to

Carter's Vineyard. Originally this was a semi-detached timber-framed thatched cottage built for farm workers, but in the years between the two World Wars, it had become derelict. When council houses became available in the 1920/30s, the farm workers left their tied cottages in favour of the council houses. No one of any consequence wished to live in a derelict cottage so it was abandoned. However this particular cottage gained a reputation of being haunted, especially during the Second World War. Strange lights and floating white apparitions were often seen and high-pitched squeals were sometimes heard. Across the field opposite was an observation post of the Royal Observer Corps. The cottage was often surveyed with field glasses and figures were seen moving about - nothing like members of the spirit world. One evening a local special constable visited the observation post and took a closer look at the cottage across the field. Some encouragement from the Observer crew persuaded him to investigate further. Creeping up to the back of the cottage he saw men in uniform cavorting with certain young ladies. Drawing himself up to his full height of five foot four inches, The constable entered the cottage with an "Ello, Ello, what's a-goin' on 'ere?" He was rescued some hours later by the Observer crew, having been de-bagged and tied to the timber frame of the cottage. Such was the laying of these particular ghosts.

Wents cottage in 2006, now renamed The Thatched Cottage.

He saw men in uniform cavorting with certain young ladies.

Peartree Cottage.

Some houses in Church Street.
Right: Scarletts.
Centre: Church Villa and Church Cottage.
Below: Bowergreen Cottage.
Bottom: Gate Cottage.

Top left and centre: The Old Workhouse.
Top right: Noakes Farm.
Above: Thrift Cottages.
Left: Parsonage Farm.

CHAPTER NINE

THE Pubs of Boxted

The Cross Inn

THE CROSS INN WAS THE FIRST OF BOXTED'S PUBLIC HOUSES and the only inn. It was first recorded in 1784 and formerly known as the Dog and Partridge. The house is thought to have been built towards the end of the 16th Century, and started trading as an alehouse in 1600. The property belonged to the Rivers Hall estate and was rented (copyhold) by a Thomas Boniface, Master of Ale and the official Ale Taster for the Parish Vestry. The building was situated at the main crossroads of the village, and was probably chosen as the first 'pub' because of its position. In the early days, perhaps because the ale was too strong, it was 'much affected' with 'excessive drunkenness' and a cage was built on the green opposite to 'restrain these minor offenders' hence giving the name to Cage Lane.

The Cross Inn 1981.

Civil War - Royalist support

At the time of the Civil War a John Fitzgibbon was the landlord. He was supposedly the illegitimate son of Lady Gibbon, lady-in-waiting to Queen Henrietta Maria, the wife of

The Cross Inn today is now private housing called Seven Gables.

Charles I. He was reputed to have been involved in the escape of Lord Goring, commander of the Royalist force which occupied Colchester, via Boxted in 1648. According to legend Fitzgibbon was captured by the Roundheads when they attacked Hillhouse Farm and the inn and 'shot to death'. His ghost is supposed to walk the grounds of the Cross each July.

In about 1750 the property was freed from copyhold to Rivers Hall, together with 30 acres of land which forms part of the playing field and council estate today. At this time it acquired the name 'Dog and Partridge', and was listed as an inn. An inn was required to give food and succour to the traveller, and stable his horse. It could also sell the new-fangled 'beer' and spirits as well as ale.

In 1850 its name was changed to The Cross, after John Cross, one of its most popular landlords. Since the 18th century to the middle of the 20th, its various landlords farmed the 30 acres of land belonging to the property. Before the 1872 Licensing laws, all the ale and beer was brewed in an outhouse, the brewhouse, at the rear of the inn. The 1872 Act prohibited 'brewing in sheds and backhouses' and the property was sold to Daniels' and Sons brewery at West Bergholt. Towards the end of the 19th Century a butcher's shop was opened in the thatched barn adjoining the inn, with a slaughterhouse next to the brewhouse.

The property was sold, modernised and opened as a restaurant in 1983 but the venture did not succeed. It has since been converted into a private house.

Cross Inn 1922.

ALE OR BEER.

The distinction between ale and lager beer is something which is not well understood. A common thought is that colour distinguishes these two styles of beer, a lager being golden, and an ale darker. While this may be true for some beers, it is not what distinguishes an ale from a lager. Basically the difference is in the yeast, an ale is produced at higher temperatures by a yeast that will float on the top during fermentation. A lager is produced at lower temperatures by a yeast that will sink to the bottom during fermentation.

Higher temperature brewing (ale) produces more fruity, floral flavours, while the cool temperature brewing (lager) subdues the formation of these flavours.

The Greyhound, Mill Road

In 1762, Boxted acquired its second public house, a beerhouse named The Greyhound, halfway along Mill Road. The property was said to have been occupied by a Timothy White-ear, a carriage builder. As a result of his occupation the pub was sometimes referred to as 'The Carpenter's Arms'. Timothy White-ear started the business as the first landlord brewing his beer in the end section of his wheelwright's shop.

Beer differed from ale in that it was flavoured with hops while ale had a longer fermentation period producing a stronger brew.

Beer for the unemployed

It is said that White-ear started the pub because of the large number of unemployed men (mostly weavers) who came to watch him at work building his carts and carriages, hoping he would employ them. Knowing that these ex-weavers had some money he thought he could open his beerhouse and make a profit from selling them beer. At least he would get them out of his workshop.

It is thought that The Greyhound closed in about 1848 when the then occupant bought a nearby small holding and transferred the pub business there, further down Mill Road, calling it 'Thatcher's'.

The Thatcher's, Mill Road

The Thatcher's was a much larger property, and as well as many outbuildings it had 25 acres of land. An outhouse was soon converted to brewing and the business became very prosperous. However, with the 1872 Act prohibiting brewing in backhouses, the property was sold to Messrs. Daniels' and Sons, Brewers of West Bergholt. The last landlord of the Thatcher's was probably the best remembered. He was one of Boxted's 'characters', the like of which will probably never be seen again. His name was William Page. A man of short stature he was soon referred to as 'Little Billy'. The selling of beer was only part of Billy's career. He was a general dealer who bought and sold anything he could lay his hands on. The Thatcher's closed in 1911.

Thatcher's mid renovation in 2006.

Fox Cottage has been a private house since 1926.

The Fox Pub (Lilley's), Church Street

TEENAGE LANDLADY

In 1871 the head of the household at Lilley's beerhouse in Church Street, later known as The Fox, was Salome Lilley aged 15. With her brothers, Abraham, aged eight, and Henry, aged two, they managed the pub until Abraham became landlord. Their father, Obadiah, had left home, and their mother had died of fever. While the property was owned by the Lilleys, the beer was supplied first by Josiah Cole of the Queen's Head, and after the 1872 Act, by the then Colchester Brewing Company. In 1905 Greene King of Bury St. Edmunds bought the property from Abraham Cole. Salome Lilley married the gardener from Boxted House.

He left almost immediately because of fighting and bad language at the bar.

In 1880 Herbert Thompson gives an account of a visit to The Fox in his book, 'Constable Country'. Arriving at The Fox in the early evening, he left almost immediately because of fighting and bad language at the bar. He visited St. Peter's Church, then returned for supper and a bed for the night. He was so impressed by a verse that hung above the bar that he included it in his book. It was addressed to non-paying customers -

'Since man to man is so unjust
No man can tell who he can trust.
I have trusted many to my sorrow
So pay today and trust tomorrow.'

The Fox closed in 1926.

The Wig and Fidgett 2005.

The Wig & Fidgett, Straight Road

IT IS THOUGHT THAT THE PRESENT WIG AND FIDGETT was built about 1855 and is still open for business today. There are many stories concerning the origin of the name. One refers to a previous hostelry, a base for smugglers, which was destroyed by fire in a raid by Customs officials (Tales of Old Boxted). Another suggests that it was used by magistrates as a courthouse. The most plausible explanation is that it derives from the names of the men who built it, Obadiah Wigg and Nathaniel Fidgett.

Like the rest of the Boxted Pubs, the Wig and Fidgett had a parcel of land belonging to the property, so its landlord was both a publican and farmer. The early ownership of the pub is not known, but towards the end of the 19th Century it was owned by Daniel and Sons of West

The name derives from the men who built it Obadiah Wigg and Nathaniel Fidgett.

Bergholt. During the economic depression that followed the First World War, one of the tenants, Bob Harris, owned a sawmill powered by a traction engine, which provided him with another source of income. Bob Harris's successor, Harry King, farmed land in Queen's Head Road. The best remembered tenant of these inter-war years was Bert Breed, an ex-Navy Chief Petty Officer. Following the Second World War, Daniel and Sons sold their brewery to Trumans of London who closed the West Bergholt brewery using the premises as a store. However, they continued to supply the tied houses with beer from their London brewery in Brick Lane. As brewing became more competitive, Trumans sold the West Bergholt property and offered the tied houses for sale. The Wig and Fidgett was sold privately, and today trades as a free house.

The Butcher's Arms, Workhouse Hill

The Butcher's Arms at the top of Workhouse Hill started trading in the late 1840s as a beerhouse. Little is known of its early landlords, but it was sold after the 1872 Act, to Cuddens, brewers of Sudbury, and then, in 1905, to Greene King of Bury St. Edmunds. This public house also had some 10 acres of land, together with a good range of premises for livestock. For some years, until its closure in 1919, it was the home of Munsons, the local carriers. The Munsons' carrier cart went to Colchester three times a week. As well as personal transport and the collection and delivery of goods, they carried bundles of tailoring from women outworkers to clothing factories in Colchester and brought back new work. With the closing of The Butcher's Arms Mr. Munson gave up his carrier business. The property is now a private house called Ramblers.

The Old Butchers Arms today.

The Queen's Head photographed in the twenties.

The Queen's Head

Mr. Cromer Cole built the property in 1851 as a farmhouse, which had quite a sizeable parcel of land adjoining, reclaimed from Boxted Heath. With the decline in farming fortunes he needed to find another source of income. His father, Josiah Cole, was an expert brewer so, in 1857, Cromer applied to the local magistrates for a licence to brew and retail beer. Part of the barn was turned into a brewhouse and the business became very prosperous with patrons coming from far and wide to sample Josiah's special beers.

JOSIAH COLE'S RECIPE FOR STRONG BEER:

Take 12 bushels of malt to the hogshead of water.
Pour the water hot, but not boiling onto the malt.
Infuse for three hours covered, mash in the first half hour and let it stand the remainder of the time.
Run it in the hops previously infused in water at the rate of ¾ lb of hops to 1 bushel of malt. Boil with wort for 2 hours from the start of the boil.
Cool a pailful to add 2 quarts of yeast which will prepare it for putting to the rest when ready the next day, but if possible, put together the same night.
Turn as usual. Cover the bung hole with paper when the beer has done working and when it has stopped have ready 1½ lbs of hops dried before the fire, put in bung hole and fasten it up.
Let it stand 12 months in the cask before drinking.
Beer is best if brewed in March.

Although Cromer called his property The Queen's Head, it was often called simply Cromer's. At one time, beer brewed at the Queen's Head was sold to both The Fox and Butcher's Arms.

Following Cromer Cole's death, his son-in-law, Robert Leech, became landlord. When the licensing Act of 1872 became law, the beer was supplied first by the Colchester Brewing Company of East Hill, Colchester, then by Oliver's of Sudbury and eventually by Greene King of Bury St. Edmunds. After the death of Robert Leech, his son-in-law, Henry Denny, became landlord for the next 26 years. His widow, Mary Ann Denny, held the licence for a time before it passed to her son-in-law, Harvey Carter. In 1958 Harvey's son, Douglas, became the last licensee of the Queen's Head.

The Fruitpicker's Pub

The outstanding period of prosperous trade for the Queen's Head was in the 1920/30s when fruitpickers from London came to work in the orchards of Mr. Denis Carter at Hill Farm. The horse meadow alongside the pub was opened, and beer was served through the windows of the pub. Over 200 Londoners crowded the approaches, and for the fruitpicking season, the Queen's Head had a full lorry load of beer every week.

A second era of prosperity came during the American occupation of the local airfields during World War II. Although the supplies of beer were rationed, it was possible, with some local brewing knowledge, to supplement supplies. After the war the pub obtained a licence to serve wines and spirits and trade remained good until the coming of television. Customers came in later and later, and it was only at weekends that the pub was busy. The drink drive legislation restricted trade still further but it was the Public Health Acts of the 1960s, which specified indoor toilets and washing facilities for all public houses which proved its end. The Queen's Head only had cesspool drainage and the space needed to build indoor toilets would have reduced the size of the drinking area to uneconomic proportions. In 1970, it was decided to close and de-licence the property and sell it as a private house, which later became a nursing home. The original house has since been demolished.

For the fruit picking season the Queen's Head had a full lorry load of beer every week.

CHAPTER TEN

BOXTED Tales

Smugglers

MANY OF THE FOLK TALES DATING FROM THE 1840S suggest that Boxted was home to a band of smugglers. The 1840s, often called the 'hungry forties' because of the hardships ordinary people endured, seemed to have bypassed Boxted. Many of the surrounding villages did not share Boxted's good fortune which prospered from the generosity of William Fisher Hobbs. William's wife, Edith Hobbs, (hence Fisher Hobbs) came from a wealthy family in Earls Colne. Unfortunately her brother, Justin, was arrested by Customs Officers whilst ferrying brandy across the Dengie marshes. Fortunately he provided a sufficient excuse for being there and the case was dropped. The Customs Officer based at Stratford St. Mary often dined at Boxted Lodge, the home of the Fisher Hobbs. For some reason the officer was summarily removed from Stratford and rumour has it that he was imprisoned in Pentonville.

Another local story concerning smugglers centres around the origin of the name of the Wig and Fidgett pub. The pub at that time may have been at the northern extremity of the present property beside the lane. The timber-framed thatched pub was occupied by a Captain Harwich who ran a band of smugglers carrying contraband from the Stour to Boxted. When the coast was clear of Customs Officers and he wanted the men to muster at his home he would put his wig in the front window of the house.

While the officers were in the area he would put his 'fidgett', a wig stand, on the same window as a warning.

The smugglers reversed the shoes on the pony's feet.

In the thatched barn adjoining the house he kept a number of ponies. The horses were only kept in the barn when required, otherwise they were stabled at different points throughout the parish. When a 'job' was to be done The smugglers reversed the shoes on the ponies' feet so that, when they went towards the Stour, the hoofprints suggested that they were moving in the opposite direction. The smuggled goods, mainly brandy, were brought up the river from Manningtree in rowing boats; unloaded in the boathouse at Valley Farm, Langham and then transported by pony to the barn at the Wig & Fidgett. When the coast was clear the contraband was transported along the 'Harwich Line' to Holly Cottage, Great Horkesley where it was hidden in the roof.

Captain Harwich lit a train of gunpowder.

This practice seems to have prospered for some years until one dark November evening, when the 'Wig' barn was full of brandy, Customs Officers surrounded the property. While the officers banged on the door, Captain Harwich lit a train of gun powder that led to a cask of brandy. He took some time to unbolt the door to the officers before the whole barn went up in a roar of flames. The officers stepped back in shock and the wily old captain escaped between their legs.

The field opposite the pub is still called 'Harwich Line'.

Dealers

Prior to the auction markets most farm produce, particularly livestock, was bought from the farmers and sold on to potential customers by dealers. There were several different type of dealer, each specialising in a particular commodity - horse dealers, cattle dealers, pig and poultry dealers - and general dealers. These men would buy anything from a pin to a traction engine, and sell anything from a chalice to a chamber pot.

Boxted had one such dealer, Mr. William Page, known as 'Little Billy'. Mr. Page was landlord of the Thatcher's pub in Mill Road. On an August day in 1905 'Little Billy' attended a house sale at Great Horkesley and, being the only dealer present, he had a field day buying almost everything available. So much so that his cart was unable to carry all his purchases and he had to solicit the help of a local furniture remover with a two-horse van. This gentleman, nicknamed 'Long-un' as he stood 6ft. 3ins, knew little of Billy or he may have turned down the commission.

These men would buy anything from a pin to a traction engine and sell anything from a chalice to a chamber pot.

The goods were loaded into the van and Billy and Long-un set off for the Thatcher's. Having unloaded the goods from the van to the barn at the rear of the Thatcher's, Billy called out to Long-un "Come on here, Long-un, you better come inside, have a drink and I'll square up with you."

They both went into the pub where Billy produced half a pint of small beer for Long-un and asked him how much for his services. After some deliberation Long-un said "Well, Billy, as it's you and you have given me half a pint of diluted gnat's water to drink, I shall want two shillings from you."

> "You b***** rogue,"answered Billy "Yew ont git nawthin like that out of me."
> He put his hand in his pocket and gave Long-un a sixpence.
> "You twisting little bastard Billy, I shall want more than this" and he threw the sixpence on the floor.
> "Ah, Long-un," said Billy "that's all yew'll git so yew might as well pick it up and be on your way."
> In a foul temper Long-un snatched up the sixpence and left.

Little Billy then gave an account of the affair to his customers explaining what a clever man he was and that he paid people what he liked. That night Little Billy went to bed very satisfied with his day's work.

At the crack of dawn the next morning Billy went to examine his goods and plan the sale of them for maximum profit. Opening the barn door his jaw dropped in disbelief on seeing the barn completely empty with the exception of one chamber pot. Long-un had loaded all Billy's goods into his van during the night and driven them off.

Billy took a closer look at the chamber pot which was an 'eye' pot having an eye painted inside with the following jingle inscribed around the eye 'If you wash me well and keep me clean, I will not tell what I have seen'. Attached to the handle of the pot was a note from Long-un which read 'Yew ain't seen nawthen yet'.

> 'If you wash me well and keep me clean I will not tell what I have seen'.

Fred Smith

In these times, when we are so casual about the prospect of putting a man on Mars or travelling to Australia in less than a day, there is a tendency to forget how very different were the lives of our grandparents.

Fred Smith tells a traumatic tale of his birth in September 1927 when the bed his mother was lying in fell through the floor of the thatched cottage to the room below. Even this did not hasten Fred's birth so his father had to cycle to get the nurse from Dedham, only to find that she was attending a case in Ardleigh. He cycled on to collect her, before the pair made it back to Mile End Road, where Fred was delivered.

The bed fell through the floor to the room below.

As a young lad Fred would cycle to North Hill to collect the newspapers to distribute throughout the village by 11am. He would then set off again selling vegetables from the farm.

When Severalls Hospital was being built in 1913 bricklayers and other labourers were employed on a daily basis. Some men would think nothing of walking from Clacton to Severalls for a day's wage in spite of the fact that, if work was scarce, they would have made a fruitless journey of 34 miles.

John's Flood

1928 was one of Boxted's wettest years that resulted in long delays in farm work, but during the short summer, the bus operator, Norfolk's of Nayland, ran trips to the local seaside in their newly-acquired motor bus. On one of these trips a young Elsie King had enjoyed herself so much that she tried to persuade her father to join her on a later excursion. Her father, who had never been out of Boxted in the previous 20 years, explained that they were too far behind with the farm work for him to contemplate such a trip.

Elsie continued to nag her father until he relented saying that he would ask 'The Master' if he could have a day off for the trip. The next day he duly asked 'The Master' if he could have the following Tuesday off as 'his gal Elsie' wanted him to go to the seaside with her. 'The Master' pondered a while before replying.

> "Yes, John, you can have the day off to the seaside on Tuesday - but on one condition."
> "What's that, Master?" said John.
> "That you tell me all about it when you get back."
> "That I will, that I will," replied John.

The following Tuesday Elsie and her father boarded the bus for Clacton. John was fascinated to see the progress of farm work in the Tendring Hundred. When they arrived in Clacton John could not be persuaded to go on the beach. They had lunch at a café on the front and walked round Clacton before joining the bus for the return journey.

The following day John went to the farmhouse to report on his day out.

"Ah, John, what was it like then?" asked 'The Master'.

"Well," replied John "it was all very good. They old boys in the Tendring Hundred ain't as far forward as we."

"Yes, but what about the seaside?" asked 'The Master'.

"It's like this 'ere, Master. We had a nice dinner in the town but, yer know, there's acres and acres of water and how the hell they're going to drain it off, I don't know."

Opposite: Morning sunshine through the poplars at Cheshunts. (W. Barclay 2004).

Index

D

E

F